EVERYBODY'S BUSINESS

EVERYBODY'S BUSINESS

by
Abba P. Lerner

MICHIGAN STATE UNIVERSITY PRESS

Copyright © 1961
Michigan State University Press

Library of Congress Card Catalog Number:
61-16931

Manufactured in the United States of America

CONTENTS

I.	Economics Is About People	1
II.	What Is a Fair Price?	7
III.	What Is the "Correct" Price?	14
IV.	What Is a Fair Wage?	20
V.	What Is Wrong With Monopoly?	27
VI.	What Would We Do Without the Speculator?	32
VII.	The Middleman and the Middle Class	41
VIII.	When Is a Business a Racket?	49
IX.	Economic Democracy (or, The Market and the Ballot)	59
X.	How the Money Goes Round—Prosperity, Depression, Inflation	68
XI.	Sellers' Inflation and Inflationary Depression	81
XII.	Rich Man, Poor Man—How Much Inequality Do We Need?	93
XIII.	The National Debt—Do We Owe It to Ourselves?	104
XIV.	Why Taxes?	115
XV.	Political Economy or the Use of Economics	126

PREFACE

This book started as a series of ten radio talks at Roosevelt University in Chicago around 1950 when I was Professor of Economics at that institution. The revision, translation and expansion of these talks into fifteen chapters of readable material is due mainly to John Gallagher's insistent prodding and meticulously critical editing while he was managing editor of the Michigan State University Press. Any imperfections in the clarity of presentation are due only to his exhausting my patience and to my obstinately crying "enough already." I am also grateful to COMMENTARY and to THE AMERICAN SCHOLAR for permission to make use of articles of mine they have published.

Although the book is intended in the first place for the general reader who has not taken any courses in economics, as well as for use in secondary schools and adult education classes, I have not kept away from the controversial. For this reason, among others, I believe the book will also be of interest to advanced students and even to teachers of economics in the universities.

ABBA P. LERNER
Michigan State University
October 1961

CHAPTER I

ECONOMICS IS ABOUT PEOPLE

Every infant believes that the universe exists for his own special pleasure. Too soon he learns that there are other persons also to be served. Before he can properly adjust himself to this sad discovery, he is told in kindergarten that the farmer milks cows so that children can have milk, that the miner digs coal so that houses can be warm, and that the cheerful locomotive engineer drives trains in order to help boys and girls to go on holidays. But one day he finds out that farmers, miners, and engineers are less concerned with providing good things for boys and girls than with the money they earn by working. This comes as a great shock but still greater is the shock of discovering that even if the miner or other worker wants to work at making or growing things that boys and girls like, he cannot work unless someone makes a profit from employing him.

By now the disillusioned young man is ready to denounce the society in which he lives and to declare himself for another form of social organization in which production is "for use and not for profit." His favorite story is of a visitor from Mars who is told that on earth no one is in charge of seeing that important things get done. Only that gets done, whether useful or not, which yields a *profit*, so that naturally all is chaos. The horrified Martian quickly flies back home to Mars.

While preaching this parable, the young man will be sipping his coffee, the radio turned low, comfortably seated near a well-stocked refrigerator in a warm elevator apartment, with hundreds of thousands of items for him to drink or wear or read or play with, waiting to be picked up at nearby stores or to be delivered to him in response to a telephone call! So accustomed is he to having available for his use the products and services of hundreds of thousands of people throughout the world, from the growers of his coffee to the ever ready telephone operator, that he is not even aware of them. He thus can deny the existence of the machinery that furnishes him with the highest standard of living the world has ever known. He fails to realize that the Martian *would* notice the machinery, and be very much impressed by it, and that it would not be the terrestrial society that the Martian would consider crazy, but the storyteller.

The machinery that the young man fails to see when it is working well, and is so ready to demolish as soon as it works imperfectly, is the *economic* machinery of the society. When something goes wrong with the machinery we have economic problems. We also have economic problems when the machinery is working perfectly, but there is a powerful tendency for non-economists to blame the economic machinery for *all* problems let alone economic problems. This is natural because economic problems do not concern only economists. Everybody is vitally concerned with rising and falling prices, with scarcities and gluts, with good and poor opportunities for profits and jobs. But the economist has a distinctive approach to such problems.

Many consider the distinguishing feature of economics to be a deep, dark pessimism. Indeed, economics used to be known as the "dismal" science; it was believed to consist almost entirely of methods of proving that there was no cure for poverty, that the poor will always be with us. The dismal lesson of the dismal science was that if anything did reduce poverty—say an innovation or an investment that increased production or a philanthropic transfer of income from the relatively well-to-do to the poor—the benefits could only be temporary. For with less starvation and disease, fewer people would die young, and more children would be born and survive to become parents. The population would multiply. But, as Malthus pointed out more than a century ago, there would be no corresponding increase in natural resources or productive equipment to go with the extra workers, so that population would outstrip production. Output per head would fall and keep falling until the poor were just as hungry and sick as before. Only when the previous degree of starvation, disease, and mortality has been restored would the population stop growing. Ironically, because of the increase in production, or the transfer of income to the poor, there would be even more poor people than before.

This is indeed no abstract theory but an accurate description of

ECONOMICS IS ABOUT PEOPLE

how, in most parts of the world, the growth of population still defeats every attack on poverty. But economics does not stop with painting this depressing picture. It goes on to point out that here, and in other western countries, increases in productivity are *not* negated by numbers. Population does not grow to the point where it comes to be limited by starvation and disease. Instead it is limited at an earlier point by the decisions of parents not to have so many children. Hence, we in the West enjoy enormous improvements in health and living conditions. The lesson taught by economics is that other countries could do likewise either by raising output more rapidly or by keeping down the rate of population growth, or better still, by both measures.

Economics could with more justice be accused, not of pessimism, but of over-optimism. Usually it is the economist who comes up with projects for making the world better and happier; and the political scientists, psychologists, sociologists and politicians are the ones who maintain, often with good reason, that the economist's optimistic projects are impracticable because of the ignorance, obstinacy, and laziness of the people who have to carry them out.

But while essentially optimistic, economics is not magic and cannot pull rabbits out of a hat. Economists are often asked how one gets rich—how does one make a million dollars. The economist may say that if he knew how to make a million dollars he would not be a college professor. But this is not very funny and probably not even true. If he is a good professor he is probably one of the lucky people who enjoy their work so much that they would continue to do it even if they did not need the pay. Indeed if he had a million dollars he might even do a better job just because he would not be financially dependent on it. But actually, economics cannot show anyone how to make a million dollars. It cannot show you how to become richer than your neighbor, which is what is usually meant by "making a million dollars," because economics is about *everybody,* including your neighbor, and it is transparently impossible for you to become richer than your neighbor while he becomes richer than you.

Perhaps this is why economics often seems cold and impersonal. It is just as much about your neighbor and his neighbor and even complete strangers as it is about you. It is concerned not just with *your business*, but with *everybody's business;* and everybody minds his own business so closely that everybody's business becomes *nobody's business*. The economist does not take you to his heart to the exclusion of your neighbor. Economics consists of studying how all the things that *people in general* want are produced and made available to them, and how this might be done better.

Yet, the economist is not really interested in technology, in how a particular article is produced. He leaves this to the technician who, for his part, asks no questions as to whether the right article is being produced. The economist however *is* interested in whether the manufacturer or the farmer is producing the right things. The "right things" are what the consumer wants most. No matter how skillfully, how efficiently, or even how economically the manufacturer produces, say, a surrey with a fringe on top, if the consumer would rather have an outboard motorboat that could be made from the same productive resources, the economist is unhappy because the consumer's preferences are being disregarded. The important words, therefore, in the definition at the end of the previous paragraph are "the things that the people in general want" with the emphasis on "people."

Closely related to the charge that economics is cold and impersonal are the charges that it is awfully complicated and that it is boring. Economics *is* complicated. In any economic problem one has to take account of many things. When more than a certain number must be kept in mind, the untrained reader gets confused. But if the economist sticks to the essence of the argument, leaving out complications until the core has been grasped by the reader, he is criticized for being abstract. If the economist cannot generalize for fear of being abstract, and if he is forbidden to particularize lest he complicate things, then he simply cannot win.

It is also true that many, if not most, books on economics are boring. But this is only because their authors do not make it clear that they are talking about people. Sometimes it seems as if the author himself was not really thinking about people, in which case nothing can be done by the reader. But almost any book on economics can become exciting if the reader asks himself often enough: "What difference does it make to people?—to what people want? to what people get? to what people do?"

ECONOMICS IS ABOUT PEOPLE

The economist is not primarily interested in corporations, or cooperatives, or trade unions, or private enterprise, or government enterprise, or government regulation of private enterprise, though, to be sure, he talks a lot about them. These are all *things,* not people. They are just organizational machinery or devices—ways in which people get together to produce, transport, and distribute goods and services.

Nor is the economist ultimately concerned with such phenomena as prices, or production, or sales of goods and services. The impression that he is springs from a misunderstanding of his language. He will say, for instance, that when there is an excessive money expenditure or a shortage of supply, prices will rise. But this is only shorthand—a time-saving metaphor which must not be taken literally. Prices, unlike people, cannot make decisions. A price cannot rise unless a seller and a buyer agree on a higher price.

Unfortunately, metaphorical statements are on occasion taken literally. This leads not only to nonsensical economic theory, but to bad economic policy. For example, the United States in 1934 reduced the gold content of the dollar, expecting the devaluation to make prices rise in about the same proportion. Had our policy makers asked themselves why devaluation should induce buyers and sellers to agree on higher prices, they would not have been so surprised when prices did not rise. The lesson is clear. Whenever it is stated that some occurrence would make prices rise or cause output to shrink, one must always ask how it would cause people to agree on higher prices or to reduce output. If the answer is not clear, the statement is suspect, no matter how logical, high-sounding, proper, traditional, or self-evident it may appear.

And by people I mean individuals—men, women, or children into whose eyes I can look and whose hand I can shake—not "Society." The economist does speak about "social interest," but this again is only a metaphor. It simply means that what one individual does is of importance to the other individuals that make up the society. To believe that "Society" exists in a sense apart from the individuals that comprise it is nonsense.

The same holds true for words like nation, class, city, or neighborhood. They are shorthand descriptions of organizations and sometimes of the groups of people who establish governments, political parties, clubs, trade unions, or manufacturers' associations. Such organizations are created only to serve the interests of the members; individuals are not created to serve the organizations. Some individuals may sacrifice themselves for, say, a nation, but it makes sense to do so only if the sacrifice is more than offset by benefits to the other members of the group. To sacrifice the people for the sake of an organization or movement itself is the root madness of idolatry or totalitarianism. To reiterate, organizations are only machinery for helping people to get what they want.

Not that machinery is unimportant. Our economy couldn't exist without organizational machinery. But we must not make too much either of the machinery or of its flaws.

Failure to understand the machinery, as by the young man in our initial parable, predisposes one to an exaggerated notion of its flaws, and of the benefits to be derived from replacing it with almost any alternative—usually some "planned economy." On the other hand, to over-estimate the effectiveness of the machinery leads one to resist changes for the better. Economics opens our eyes to the effectiveness as well as to the limitations, both of the existing machinery and of suggested improvements or replacements. It gives us *balance* on this vital matter.

CHAPTER II

WHAT IS A FAIR PRICE?

Whether we think a price "fair" usually depends on whether we are paying or receiving it. When buying, we tend to think a price too high; when selling, we tend to think it too low. Since there must be a buyer whenever there is a seller, and *vice versa,* it follows that there can rarely be agreement on the fairness of any price. Furthermore, since a price cannot be at once both raised and lowered, it would seem impossible to make any price fairer than it already is.

Complaints about unfairness are most frequent when prices change. If a price is maintained for a long time, people become accustomed to it. Then when something raises it, buyers cry "unfair;" if something lowers it, the sellers complain. A price may therefore seem fair only because we have become accustomed to it. But we can become accustomed to bad things as well as to good things. Continuing a customary price may simply mean that there is no new injustice; the price may have been unjust from the beginning.

It might be thought that a simple test of the fairness of a price is to see whether the seller's profit is "reasonable." But this does not help us very much, not only because what is "reasonable" is no clearer than what is "fair," but because there is the further problem of drawing the line between profits and costs. This is by no means easy.

Whenever there is an opportunity for making a profit, the owner of the opportunity can hire it out for a rental approximately equal to the expected profit. To the person paying for the opportunity, the rent is a cost, just like any other cost he meets in running a business; so that he can honestly say that he is not getting the profit—he is handing it over—or almost all of it—as rent to the owner. To the owner, the rent constitutes a return on capital, and rent always represents a "reasonable" return on capital. This is because capital value is calculated by finding the sum on which the rental *would* be a reasonable return. There is nothing crooked about this calculation. Indeed, there is no other way to calculate it, for a capital value is nothing but a "reasonable" or "fair" valuation of the privilege of receiving a rent. But have the profits then disappeared up someone's sleeve?

Suppose I own a mine from which coal can be taken at a cost per ton which is considerably less than the price at which it can be sold. I make a large profit. But suppose I consider renting the mine to you for $50,000 a year. You would be glad to pay that rent if it is less than the difference between the cost of digging the coal and the proceeds for which the coal can be sold. Your profit would then be what is left after you pay the rent on top of all the other costs that I also would have had to pay. If your profits were still high, I could raise the rent; and if you should object, someone else would be willing to pay it, as long as I do not ask so much that the mine could be operated only at a loss. There is no large or abnormal or unreasonable profit in the mine for you.

If the rent is $50,000 a year and the current rate of return on investments is five per cent per annum, then the capital value of the coal mine will be a million dollars. The earnings on it are by no means exorbitant; $50,000 is precisely five per cent of a million dollars. If the rent were $100,000, the mine would be worth two million dollars; and the return would still be a reasonable five per cent. No matter how much rent I charge, it can never be more than a reasonable return on the capital value. Moreover, the capital value of the mine is reasonable too. It is no more than what I would be able to get for the mine from a buyer who in turn would be making a reasonable five per cent on his investment. Whatever the price, nobody seems to be making an unreasonably high profit. We cannot, therefore, use these grounds for complaining that the price of coal is unreasonably high and unfair to the buyers of coal.

This illustration does not, of course, prove that the price of coal, or the rent of the mine, or its selling price, is fair. It only shows that we cannot tell whether a price is fair or not by trying to find out whether profits are "reasonable."

Obviously, we have not reached the heart of the problem. We cannot in fact say anything meaningful about the fairness of prices

WHAT IS A FAIR PRICE?

until we are clear about the purpose of prices in our economic system.

The purpose of prices is to help our economic system make available to every consumer what he prefers without diminishing the satisfaction of other consumers. It is important to pay attention to the stipulation: *"without diminishing the satisfaction of other people."* It is no trick at all to improve the position of one consumer by taking what he wants away from someone else, perhaps by force. But to see that each consumer gets what he prefers *without* depriving anyone else can be achieved only through the most efficient production and allocation of goods and services and the most efficient determination of what goods and services should be produced. This is just what is achieved through the proper use of money, prices, and markets.

There are two ways in which prices help achieve efficiency. The first concerns the *allocation* of the *currently available* goods and services, (including those whose production is near completion). The only question here is, who should get how much of which goods or services—how to allocate them efficiently among the consumers. The second concerns the *production* of goods and services—what quantities of what goods and services should be produced.

The allocation of goods and services among consumers is inefficient if a reallocation could make some consumers better off without making others worse off. Such reallocation is possible if some goods and services have gone to "the wrong place." The clearest case of an inefficient allocation is when I have something you prefer while you have what I prefer. The reallocation that consists of a simple exchange benefits both of us without hurting anyone. The exchange puts each item in "the right place"—namely in the possession of the person who prefers it to the alternative.

The "right place" for any item is, therefore, in the hands of a consumer who wants it at least as much as anyone else, in the sense that he would pay at least as much for it as anyone else. If anyone else, anywhere, is willing to pay more for it, then he is the one who should have it.

This is where prices come in. Prices can bring about the most efficient allocation of goods and services, sending every item to "the right place." The conditions for achieving this are simple: at any time, the price of every item must be the same for everyone, and everyone must be free to buy as much as he wants of any item at that price. Every consumer then refrains from buying goods and services that he does not consider worth the price. He spends his money on other things or he saves it. The prices he refuses to pay can be maintained only if other consumers *are* willing to pay them. They buy what the first consumer rejects, and he gets what they reject. Everything goes to the person who is willing to give the most for it and who in this sense wants it most.

If this claim seems excessive, that is only because it appears to claim more than it actually does. We have been careful to consider only the relative importance for a consumer of two different items, or his preference between them. We have not compared the importance of the same item to two different people. It is perfectly possible for all the items considered to be more important to one consumer than to another. This will frequently be the case if one is much poorer than the other. It might then seem desirable to take one or both of the items away from the rich man and give them to the poor man. But this would not increase the efficiency of allocation; we would not be benefiting one consumer without harming another. The rich man would be harmed by this operation. Indeed, in such a one-way transfer from one individual to another we would be dealing not with consumer *preferences* as between different goods and services, but with consumer *needs* for goods and services in general. This is a problem not of allocation of goods and services but of the division of income, which is discussed in Chapter XII, "Rich Man, Poor Man."

Prices are democratic in operation. They allocate goods and services according to the preferences of the consumer, not according to the judgment of a bureaucrat or dictator. A rationing system, the only alternative to the price system, is dictatorial in that it does not allow for the satisfaction of individual preferences. Any attempt to treat different individuals differently would lead to an immediate and complete administrative breakdown. That is why there is always pressure to eliminate rationing as soon as an emergency is over.

WHAT IS A FAIR PRICE?

At any time there is only one *genuine* price possible for each item or service on the market. The genuine price is a price that clears the market. Any other price, though it may seem "fairer" to some people, is a fraud. The genuine price is sometimes condemned as "charging what the traffic can bear"—words that make most people feel they are being overcharged. But it really means nothing more than the price at which a buyer can obtain as much as he can pay for and a seller can dispose of as much as he has available. The question whether a higher or lower price would be fairer cannot even arise. A higher price would leave some of the items unsold and wasted, being nothing but a mockery to would-be sellers who cannot find customers; a lower price would constitute a mockery to those who cannot find a seller.*

After World War II, automobile manufacturers in the United States sold their automobiles to dealers for less than "what the traffic could bear." The dealer could have resold the cars at list price, say $1600, and made his customary profit. But at $1600 the public wanted more new cars than were available. The result was that one couldn't buy a new car. Only after the dealer had driven it around the block could one buy it as a second-hand car for $2200. Twenty-two hundred dollars was the "genuine" price, what the car was worth on the market and what one could have got for it by reselling it after driving it home. In selling the cars for less than what the traffic would bear, the manufacturer was in fact giving a present to the automobile dealer of $600 in addition to his customary profit.

Occasionally a dealer would sell a car to a steady customer at the list price of $1600. Such an "honest dealer" was then passing on the $600 gift to his customer, but the "genuine" price was still $2200. Even the lucky customer who got a new car for $1600 could truly say that it cost him the "genuine" price of $2200 to keep and use the car, because he could have got that price for it after driving it home. If he kept the car, it was because he valued it at more than $2200. It was just as if he had been given a cash present of $600 and had then paid $2200 for the car.

---

* "It's true," said the shopkeeper, "that our competitor down the street, who is out of stock, is selling at half our price. If we were out of stock we could sell it even cheaper. The trouble is, we have it in stock."

The black market, charging what the traffic could bear, established the genuine price of $2200, which resulted in the available cars going to the customers who needed them most, measuring "need" by the willingness and ability to pay for a new car. The "fairer" price ($1600), when it was not negated by the black market, made cars available, not necessarily to those who were prepared to pay more for them, but to old customers who may not have needed cars, but bought them because they were offered a bargain. So there was not an efficient allocation of motor cars. The gradual recognition that the black market allocated cars more efficiently, led to its being upgraded into the grey market and later the free market. This is how other rationing or price controls gave way to the free market as soon as the war emergency passed so that prices became genuine again.

When prices are genuine each consumer will increase the amount he buys of any item as long as an *additional unit* of it is more useful to him than anything else he can buy with the same money.

The usefulness of an additional unit of an item depends on how much of it the individual has to begin with. If he already has a great deal, an additional unit will be less useful to him. The usefulness to the individual of an additional unit of an item is called its *marginal utility,* and it depends on how much he has of the item. The degree to which the usefulness of additional units becomes less and less the more he has of the item is called *diminishing marginal utility*. An individual will buy more of any item if its marginal utility is greater than that of any alternative which the same money could buy. If he should discover that the marginal utility of a dollar's worth of one item is greater than that of another, he will buy more of the first and less of the second. Thus he acquires more utility at no extra cost.

The marginal utility of the first item goes down as he gets more of it, and the marginal utility of the second item goes up as he has less and less of it left. But as long as there remains any difference in the marginal utility, he will keep shifting from the item with the lower to the item with the higher marginal utility, stopping only when the difference between the marginal utilities has disappeared. The result is that each consumer buys such quantities

WHAT IS A FAIR PRICE?

of each product as makes the marginal utility of a dollar's worth of every item that he buys equal to that of a dollar's worth of every other item.[1]

When the consumer has established this relationship among the marginal utilities, he has reached an optimum allocation of his spending. However, this is possible only if the consumer has access to a market with "genuine" prices at which he can freely buy as much as he is able and willing to pay for.

[1] The marginal utility of a dollar's worth of every item of which he does not buy any at all may be less than that of the items that he does buy, but never greater. If it were, he would buy some of it and increase the amount he bought until its marginal utility was no longer greater than that of the other items bought.

CHAPTER III

WHAT IS THE "CORRECT" PRICE?

Starting out with a discussion of "fair" prices, we were led in Chapter II to give up this notion in favor of the "genuine" price which in a free market results in the most efficient allocation of the currently available consumption goods and services among the different consumers in the economy, each item going to the "right place." We may now turn to the second part of the task performed by the price mechanism; namely, determining what goods and services will be made currently available, i.e., what goods and services will be produced.

The way this works is roughly familiar to everyone. If people want a product sufficiently, they will pay enough to make its production and sale profitable. As a result, those items are produced which the public prefers. But we must consider not only *what* goods and services are produced, but *how much* of each is produced. How much of any item is produced depends on how much is sold, and that in turn depends on price.

Just as the consumer adjusts the amount he buys of any item in accordance with its price and the prices of the alternatives, so also does the producer adjust his output according to prices. There is an optimum output for every producer at which he makes the most profit. As long as the price of a product exceeds the *marginal cost*, he will increase his output. The marginal cost is the additional expense incurred in producing an additional unit of an item, or the money saved by producing a unit less of it. The excess of price over marginal cost constitutes extra profit that can be obtained by producing an extra unit. The producer will, therefore, expand as long as price remains greater than marginal cost. If marginal cost exceeds price, he will reduce output because more money is saved thereby than is lost from selling a unit less.

When producers increase output, to take advantage of an excess of price over marginal cost, the price tends to fall and the marginal

WHAT IS THE "CORRECT" PRICE?

cost tends to rise so that the gap between them diminishes. When the gap has disappeared, the expansion will stop. When producers reduce output to take advantage of an excess of marginal cost over price, the price tends to rise and the marginal cost tends to fall. The contraction will continue until this gap has disappeared (unless production reaches zero first).

The result is that the price of every item that remains in production becomes equal to the marginal cost; a dollar's worth of each product will have a marginal cost of just one dollar. In a competitive economy this means that producing an extra dollar's worth of an item uses up exactly a dollar's worth of labor, materials and other factors of production, and that producing a dollar's worth less of any product saves exactly a dollar's worth of the factors of production. When this is the case, the prices are "correct."

We have seen that if prices are "genuine" every dollar spent by a consumer buys something that is at least as useful to him as anything else he could buy for that dollar. If prices are "correct" as well as "genuine," the resources that would be saved by making one dollar's worth less of any product are never worth more than one dollar. These resources could never produce more than one extra dollar's worth of any other product, and therefore could never produce anything that the consumer prefers to what he is actually getting. *All the productive resources in the economy are being used in the most effective way to satisfy the consumer.* Any change is certain to be a deterioration. Thus, production for profit turns out to be the most efficient method of achieving production for use. If prices are "genuine," they bring about the optimum allocation of the available goods and services among consumers, and if they are also "correct," they also bring about the optimum allocation of the factors of production in making different products available.

One could say that the function of prices is to discourage consumers from using up things and to encourage producers to produce them. Consumers should be discouraged from using up available goods and services to the degree to which it is important that they be left for others to consume. This is indicated by the degree to which the other consumers bid up prices. If there is a very small supply of an item which is in great demand, it's price will be very high, which induces consumers to use it very sparingly. If an item is plentiful, the price will be low, which will discourage consumption very little, and if the item is superabundant so that it becomes a completely free good (the price is zero) then there is no discouragement at all to its consumption. The "genuine" price automatically gives just the right degree of discouragement to the consumer.

But the prices, although "genuine," may still not be "correct." For this they must be giving the proper degree of encouragement to producers so that the proper quantities of the different products have been made available by them. As long as it is possible to benefit consumers by producing less of one product and, with the resources set free, producing something else that the consumer would rather have had instead, the different products have not been produced in the proper proportions. But in a competitive economy any price greater than the marginal cost of a product encourages the producer to expand output, and any price below marginal cost is an inadequate encouragement so that the producer responds to it by contracting output. Such contractions set free productive resources to be used by the expanding producers to make more of the items with price above marginal cost—and the high price is the indication that the product is preferred by the consumer. When the gaps between marginal cost have all disappeared, no further shifting of resources to preferred products is any longer possible. The producers have been given just the right degree of encouragement and the prices are "correct" as well as "genuine."

Producers also need to be discouraged from using up resources. How much they should be discouraged depends on how much the resources are needed for other purposes, and the prices of the factors of production constitute the proper measure of this consideration. For example, if the marginal cost of a television set that sells for $150 is $100 and the marginal cost of a refrigerator that sells for $100 is also $100—if both use up the same quantity of resources for a marginal unit—there is a faulty allocation of resources. The prices are not "correct," even if they are "genuine." The consumers prefer another television set to another refrigerator. They show this by their willingness to pay more. Consumers would be better off if there were a shift of resources from refrigerators to television sets.

That shift is automatic in production for profit. Because the television set sells for more and the costs of production are the same, a shift of productive resources *pays*. Television manufacturers bid factors of production away from the refrigerator manufacturers. The shift will continue until the profit difference between making television sets and making refrigerators has been eliminated.

At this point the price of each item will be equal to its marginal cost of production; an extra dollar's worth of television sets has the same marginal cost—and uses up the same quantity of resources—as an extra dollar's worth of refrigerators and the consumer cannot be benefitted by shifting resources from one of their products to the other.

The "correct" price is one equal to the *marginal* cost—not the *average* cost (except when this turns out to be the same as the marginal cost). This mistake is easily made if we merely say that the price should correspond to the cost of production without specifying "marginal." The marginal cost is the *difference* in total cost of producing an item if one unit more or one unit less is produced. It is obtained by *subtraction*. The average cost is the *ratio* of the total cost to the number of units produced, and is obtained by *division*. For example, say I manufacture 100 units of an item for $1000. The average cost is $10. If it would cost me $1020 to make 101 units, the marginal cost is $20, and $20 is the "correct" price for the item, not $10.

Nobody has fallen into this trap of putting average for marginal cost more spectacularly than George Bernard Shaw,* when he learned that coal was being sold at a price that covered the cost of mining the hardest-to-get coal (i.e., at the marginal cost). In the coal industry the average cost is very much below the marginal cost, so that a price equal to the marginal cost results in very great profits. Bernard Shaw appears to have a moral objection to the great wealth of the coal owners derived from these profits. He thought that coal should be priced somewhere between the marginal cost and what it costs to mine the easiest-to-get coal, and plumped for the average cost plus a "reasonable" profit for the coal industry as a

---

* In his book *The Intelligent Women's Guide to Socialism*, London, 1930. This error is pointed out by Mrs. Blanco-White in a book called *The Socialist Women's Guide to Intelligence*, London, 1931.

whole. By this he proved that a good playwright can be a bad economist.

What bothered Bernard Shaw was not really the question of what is the "correct" price for coal. He was concerned with the question of the division of income or of wealth, of whether the mines should not really belong to someone else or to the community at large, or whether there should not be heavy taxes on income or on inheritance.

Pricing coal at the average cost would make it too cheap. Too much coal would be produced. If coal were sold at the average cost of $100 though the marginal cost was $200, the productive resources set free by producing $100 worth less of coal would be able to produce $200 worth of other things—housing, insulation material, refrigerators, bicycles, clothing, food, etc., and even the poorest consumer of coal would rather have two hundred dollars worth of these than the hundred dollars' worth of coal. The consumer buys the coal because he is not being discouraged sufficiently by the price of coal as compared with the prices of the alternatives. If the prices were "correct" the alternative products would not cost more than the coal and he would buy these goods instead.

To many people it seems impossible to believe that a price can be too low. Anybody who suggests that a price should be higher is looked upon as a hardhearted person who doesn't want the users of coal to have enough to keep their houses warm and do their laundry. Yet, ironically, the people who keep some prices too low damage the efficiency of the economy in exactly the same way as those who keep other prices too high. The essential thing in prices is the *relationship* among them. Whenever one price is too low, it means that other prices are too high.

Whether a distortion of the proper relationship among prices comes from some prices being held down by sentimental philanthropists or from other prices being held up by rapacious monopolists, the result is the same—overproduction and overuse of items that are relatively too cheap, and the underproduction *and* underuse of items that are relatively too dear. The concept of "fairness" is then inapplicable to prices altogether. A price is "genuine" if it clears the market. It then contributes to the efficiency of the economy in *allocating* available goods and services among consumers

WHAT IS THE "CORRECT" PRICE?

in accordance with their preferences. Prices are "correct," as well as "genuine," if they are equal to marginal costs. Prices then contribute even more to the efficiency of the economy in regulating the *production* of goods and services in accordance with consumers' preferences.

CHAPTER IV

WHAT IS A FAIR WAGE?

To say what is a fair wage is even more difficult than to say what is a fair price for other goods and services. For a wage is a price, a price paid for the commodity called labor. But people are more passionate about wages than about other prices, so that whatever I say about wages, I shall probably tread on somebody's toes.

It is frequently declared, not only by labor leaders but by other people who deal with labor problems, that labor is not a commodity. The statement certainly cannot be taken literally. A commodity is anything that is bought and sold, and labor is bought and sold every time anyone agrees to work for a certain wage. Nevertheless, "labor is not a commodity" has been adopted as a slogan by the International Labor Office, even though the chief occupation of that office is to observe the conditions under which labor is currently being sold to see that everybody gets a fair deal.

People are touchy about calling labor a commodity because they are thinking not of labor, but of laborers as human beings. They are thinking, not of the price of the factor of production called labor, but of the income of the laborers and their families, whose health and happiness are more important than any problem connected with the prices of factors of production.

This is, of course, a most respectable point of view, very close to our thesis that economics is primarily about *people,* not about prices. But prices of commodities are also of interest to economists just because they may affect the well-being of people. This is no less true of the price of labor than of the prices of lifeless wood and steel. Much can be learned that is of importance for the well-being of people by the objective study of wages as prices for the different varieties of the commodity labor, and how the proper use of this price, among other prices, can contribute to the efficiency of the economy in serving the people. The slogan "labor is not a commodity" hinders rather than helps such studies.

WHAT IS A FAIR WAGE?

Just as in the case of prices in general, we must consider not whether a wage is "fair," but whether it is "genuine" and "correct." "Fairness" it should be remembered strictly refers to the distribution of income and wealth, not to the relations between wages or between prices. The "genuine" wage is the wage that clears the market. At that wage everyone can find all the work he wants, and every employer can find all the labor he needs. There is neither involuntary unemployment nor a shortage of labor.

If a genuine wage is arbitrarily increased, with the idea of making it more "fair," unemployment will result and the wage will no longer be genuine. The manufacturer will reduce his demand for labor as he finds more ways to replace it with machinery and other factors of production which have become relatively cheaper because their prices have not risen as much as wages. Such substitution can mitigate the rise in the cost of production but cannot completely eliminate it—otherwise the labor would not have been used even before the wage was increased. With higher costs the price of the product will rise. Consumers will then buy less, less will be produced, and there will be a further reduction in employment. There will be involuntary unemployment.

Should a genuine wage be arbitrarily reduced, the employer will employ more labor instead of other factors of production. As cost of production falls, producers will want to produce and sell more. More workers will be needed on both counts, but employers will not be able to find them. There will be a labor shortage.

In the first case, the current wage becomes meaningless to those who cannot find work and in the second case to those who cannot find workers. The price mechanism fails to perform efficiently and we have the wastefulness of unemployment or of employers interfering with orderly production as they try to hire workers away from each other. The remedy is to make the wage genuine by raising it as long as the demand exceeds the supply, or lowering it as long as the supply exceeds the demand.

An unchanged wage may cease to be genuine because of a change in the demand or supply for labor. The wage may then be made genuine again by raising or by lowering it, as the occasion requires.

A depression in an industry or region may come from a change in taste. People want something else instead so they buy less of the product under consideration; fewer workers are then needed. The wage now ceases to be genuine; some workers are unemployed. In such a case reducing the wage will cure the unemployment—manufacturers will use more labor in place of other factors of production and the cost reduction will permit the price to be lowered so that consumers will buy more. The supply of labor will equal demand, in part because some workers will have moved to other occupations, and in particular into the industry producing the products *favored* by the change in taste. The new wage will be genuine.

Conversely, where the demand for the product increases, because of a change in taste, more labor will be needed and the wage will cease to be "genuine." There will be a labor shortage. The cure is for the wage to be raised. This will reduce the demand for labor. Other factors of production will be used in place of labor and the demand for the product will fall as its price is pushed up by the increased cost of production. At the same time the higher wage will attract new workers—in particular from the industry that has been hurt by the change in taste. Eventually the supply and demand for labor will be equal and the wage will be genuine again.

But when there is a *general* excess or a deficiency of demand, i.e., if there is a state of unemployment or of labor shortage in the *economy as a whole,* changing the wage does not work in the same way. The process we have just examined for making a wage genuine again, depends essentially on wages *not* being changed at the same time and in the same direction elsewhere in the economy. If other wages also rise or fall at the same time, the prices of machinery and of the other factors of production would also rise or fall; there would then be no reason for substituting labor for the other factors of production or vice versa. Nor would there be a change in sales. If all prices change in the same way there is no reason why the consumer should shift from one product to another. This is why a *general* inflation or depression constitutes a quite different kind of problem and cannot be treated by the raising or lowering of wages that is appropriate for an excess or deficiency of demand for labor in a particular industry or region. This problem of *general* inflation or depression is discussed in Chapter X, "How the Money Goes Round."

In Chapter III we saw that a "correct" price is one that bears a

WHAT IS A FAIR WAGE?

certain relationship to cost (namely equality to marginal cost) and wages constitute the central item in cost. The "correctness" of a price, therefore, may be expressed as its bearing a certain relationship to the wage. The "correctness" of a wage consists of exactly the same relationship looked from the other end, when it is seen as a relationship of the wage to the price (of the product made by the men earning the wage) instead of as the relationship of the price to the wage (earned by the men making the product). Consequently the correct price implies the correct wage and vice versa.

This is seen most clearly in the simplified case where labor is the only factor of production. Then the marginal cost of a product is the cost of additional labor needed to make an additional unit. Prices equal to this marginal labor cost are "correct," because they would lead the producers to make the items that are preferred by the consumer whenever the choice is between items that use up the same amount of labor. Only then will the alternatives have the same price, providing equal discouragement to the consumer, so that the labor will be directed by the consumer's unbiased choice of the item that gives him the greater satisfaction.

We can now formulate the rule that tells us when a wage is "correct." The extra output from employing an additional unit of labor, is called its (i.e., labor's) *marginal product* (just as the extra expenditure involved in making an additional unit of a product is called its marginal cost). When the wage equals the value of its marginal product, nothing can be gained by shifting labor to another industry, or region. The increase in output in one place would just balance the loss of output in another. The wages are "correct" because they have succeeded in guiding each unit of labor to where it can produce the most valuable product (which is the one the consumers prefer). If the marginal products are unequal in value, the wages are not "correct" because labor still needs to be shifted from where the value of its marginal product is less to where it is greater until this gap has been eliminated.

To sum up, wages must be "genuine" if we are to avoid involuntary unemployment and depression, or labor shortages and inflation. Wages must be "correct" if the economy is to produce efficiently what the consumer prefers. A correct wage equals the value of the marginal product. When every wage equals the value of its marginal product, then all prices will equal marginal cost; and not only all wages, but all prices, will be "correct."

It may be objected that if other factors of production are used together with labor in producing a product (which is normally the case), the marginal cost of the product will be geater than the cost of the extra labor because it must also include the cost of the additional quantities of these other factors of production. The same objection also applies to the calculation of marginal product. If the product is increased by adding quantities of other factors as well as of labor, one is not justified in calling the whole increase in product the marginal product of labor. Some of the credit must go to the extra quantities of the other factors. Consequently, it may be argued, it no longer follows that the marginal product is simply the other side of the marginal cost and this upsets the pretty symmetry between the correct price being equal to the marginal cost, and the correct wage being equal to the marginal product.

This objection can be met by speaking of the marginal *net* product instead of the marginal product. The value of the marginal net product of labor is the value of the extra product *minus* the extra outlay on the factors cooperating with the labor. Only the difference between these two is what can properly be attributed to labor, and this is what is the inverse of the marginal cost of the product. For example, suppose that one extra unit of labor with a price (wage) of $2 is used together with an extra $1's worth of other factors of production and the outcome is three more units of product whose price is $1 per unit. Then the price is correct because it is equal to the marginal cost ($1 per unit is the same as $3 per three units) and the wage is correct because it is equal to its marginal net product ($3 of product minus $1 of other factors employed).

Our original proposition that the wage is correct if it is equal to the marginal product will then not stand up unless the marginal product (the difference in product that would result from changing *only* the quantity of labor, leaving all the other factors unchanged), happens to be equal to the marginal net product. Fortunately, this is indeed the case as can easily be shown. As soon as the producer becomes aware of a difference (or gap) between the marginal product and the marginal net product, he will take steps to

WHAT IS A FAIR WAGE?

eliminate it. This is what he will do. If the marginal product is less than the marginal net product he will decrease output by the method of dismissing labor alone (losing the marginal product), and he will increase output by the other method, namely, by increasing labor together with the accompanying factors (so as to enjoy the greater marginal *net* product). By this means he can increase his profits, obtaining the same output at a reduced total outlay or an increased output for the same total outlay. The profits come from his having changed his method of production to a more efficient one. The difference or gap between the marginal product and the marginal net product of labor is a signal of a faulty ratio between the factors. As he improves the ratio by substituting other factors for labor, the marginal product will rise and the marginal net product will fall until the gap between them has disappeared. The producer will then keep to the new and more efficient ratio between labor and the other factors. The marginal product of labor will then be equal to the marginal net product of labor and both will be equal to the "correct" wage.

The same argument will apply in reverse to the case where the marginal net product is found to be *less* than the marginal product. An objection of exactly the same nature may also be directed at the case (also quite normal) where there is more than one product. If several outputs are increased together it is inappropriate to attribute the total increase in cost to only one of the products. The answer to this is exactly analogous too. One must speak of the marginal *net* cost of the increase in one of the products. This is the total increase in cost *minus* the value of the other increased products. The "correct" price of the product is then one that is equal to the marginal *net* cost. But it can be shown, again in perfect analogy, that a difference between the marginal cost and the marginal net cost is a sign of an uneconomic or inefficient ratio between the different products, and that as soon as the producer has corrected this (and thereby increased his profits), the difference will have disappeared and the correct price will be equal to the marginal cost as well as to the marginal *net* cost.

Even with both "genuine" and the "correct" wages, however, there would not necessarily be a "fair" division of the social product. Some people would be receiving large incomes because they happened to own coal or uranium mines, or highly valued skills or personal gifts, say, for making people laugh. Other people, just as deserving, will not be able to earn an adequate income at the "correct" wage for any work they may be able to do. This problem doubtless lies in the minds of persons who are concerned about a "fair" wage. But this problem is not related to wages, but to the *distribution* of income and wealth, which is discussed in Chapter XII.

CHAPTER V

WHAT IS WRONG WITH MONOPOLY?

So far, we have been taking for granted another condition necessary for the optimum allocation of resources. Prices and wages cannot be genuine if there is any kind of restriction on the movement of products or factors of production. Each product must be free to go to the consumer who will pay the most for it and each factor of production must be free to go where it can earn the greatest pay. It will, however, not be necessary for us to examine restrictions on both factors and products. A restriction on the movement of products can be considered as an indirect restriction on the movement of factors of production so that it will suffice to consider only the latter.

The most obvious restrictions on the movement of factors of production are those imposed by law, by violence (or threats of violence), or by secrecy. Not quite so obvious but nonetheless real a restriction on the movement of labor is a *minimum wage,* whether enforced by law or otherwise, that keeps a wage higher than it otherwise would be. A minimum wage has the effect of keeping out workers whom it does not pay to employ at the prescribed wage; hence they must remain unemployed or find work in other occupations or areas where they are less productive. The proponents of the minimum wage are so certain that it benefits almost everybody that they have often succeeded in persuading even the excluded victims that they are really beneficiaries who happen to be unlucky.

A subtler kind of restriction results from imperfection of competition. A manufacturer adjusts his output so as to make the price equal to the marginal cost (and thereby correct) only if competition is so perfect that he regards the market price as independent of the volume of his own sales and therefore equal to "marginal revenue"—the increase in his total revenue from selling a unit more. If a manufacturer can sell 51 units at the same price, say $1, as when he sells 50 units, the marginal revenue—the difference between $51 and $50 is the same as the price. But if we have monopoly or imperfect competition, sales do significantly affect the price and marginal revenue is no longer equal to it. If the price falls from $1 to 99¢ when he sells a unit more, total revenue increases from $50 to $50.49 (for 51 units at 99¢ each) and the marginal revenue is only 49¢. It is 50¢ less than the price (99¢) because of the 50 pennies he loses from having to sell the other 50 units at 99¢ each instead of $1.

But the manufacturer is really interested in the marginal revenue, or what he gets, not in the price or what the consumer pays. Since he gets only 49¢ out of selling an extra unit it does not pay him to go beyond the point where the marginal cost of producing it reaches 49¢. The price, being greater than the marginal revenue, is greater than the marginal cost and is therefore not correct. By the same token the wage is less than the value of the marginal product and also not correct. The effect of the monopoly or imperfection of competition is that output is restricted and labor and other factors of production are kept out just as effectively as by a more open form of restriction.

A similar restriction takes place if there is imperfect competition in *buying*, which economists call monopsony. The manufacturer then has to figure that an increase in his work force (or other factors of production) raises the wage (or factor price) and this makes his marginal cost greater than the wage. If the wage rises from $1 to $1.01 per hour when he hires 51 workers instead of 50, the marginal cost of something that uses up one hour of labor is not $1.01 but $1.51. It is greater than the wage by the 50¢ he loses from having to pay a penny more per hour to each of the original 50 workers when he hires 51 instead of 50. The manufacturer will still adjust production so as to make his marginal cost equal to his marginal revenue. But now the wage ($1.01) is less than the marginal cost ($1.51) and therefore less than the marginal revenue and less than the value of the marginal product. The wage is below the "correct" wage, the price is above the "correct" price and output and employment are restricted below the correct or competitive level.

If there is monopoly as well as monopsony, the price will be

WHAT IS WRONG WITH MONOPOLY?

doubly above the "correct" price, the wage will be doubly below the "correct" wage, and employment and output will be doubly below the "correct" level. This is the fundamental evil of monopoly or monopsony. There is too little of the particular economic activity—always judging by the preferences of consumers as shown by their willingness to pay.

If there is too little of any particular economic activity this means that too little of the factors of production are being used in it, and it follows that too much of them are left for use elsewhere. The distortion caused by monopoly or monopsony (or any other restriction) is *relative*. If one dollar's worth of a factor could add two dollars' worth of product in the restricted field, what is needed is an expansion of the restricted field, making use of factors that are currently producing something worth less than $2. If any of the same factors are being used in fields where there is no restriction, the value of their marginal product will be equal to the price of the factor. They will then be producing goods worth only $1 and they should be shifted to the restricted field where their marginal product is worth $2. The argument is, of course, stronger and the waste more obvious if the excluded factors are unemployed and producing nothing at all. But there is waste even if they do find employment elsewhere because they will in general be producing something needed less urgently than what they could have produced in the restricted industry.

The qualification "in general" is necessary because the alternative employment found by the excluded factors may be in a field where there is an even greater restriction. In that case the first restriction may result in resources being moved out to a field where they will be producing things that are *more* urgently needed—just because *their* supply is being even more stringently restricted.

Where we have several equally restricted fields there is nothing to be gained by shifting factors between them. If one dollar's worth of a factor could add, say, two dollars' worth of product in either of two fields of activity, transferring a unit from one such field to the other does no good. There is a loss of two dollars' worth of product in one field and an equal gain in the other field. Only an expansion in *both* fields, using factors from less restricted fields, where their marginal product is lower, is of any use.

It appears from this analysis that efficiency would not be impaired if there were the same degree of monopolistic or monopsonistic or other restriction in *every* part of the economy, because there would then be *the same ratio* everywhere between each factor and the value of its marginal product. It would then be impossible to increase the product by shifting factors from any place to another!

It is, however, impossible for the same degree of restriction to be operative in every part of the economy. It is conceivable that every employer, in maximizing profit under imperfect competition, would make the value of the marginal product greater than the wage in just the same degree—making it, say, twice as great as the wage, paying a $1 wage when the value of the marginal product was $2. But if workers could work on their own and sell the product *directly* to the consumers, their "direct" output would naturally keep expanding as long as the value of the "direct" marginal product was greater than $1, and would stop only when the direct marginal product had fallen to $1. Our conditions for social efficiency (i.e., the same ratio everywhere between factor prices and value of marginal product) would not be met. The ratio would be 1:2 in all the factories, but 1:1 for direct production outside the factories.

It is possible in some cases for the 1:2 ratio to be imposed on direct producers by taxes or by regulations to hold up the price or hold down the output. But there are important cases where this cannot be done.

Where a producer does something for himself or for his family or friends in his own house or garden, he will extend his activity up to the 1:1 ratio point where the usefulness of the product is no longer any greater than the wage. If the factory wage is $1 an hour he will prefer to work for himself as long as he produces something worth more than $1 by gardening, house repair, baby sitting or any other kind of unrestricted, untaxed, and possibly even untaxable, activity that he can carry on at home. But in the factory, although the wage is only $1, his marginal product is worth $2. The restrictions are wasting social output by inducing men to work at home where they can produce only one dollar's worth of product when it is *technically* possible for them, by working in the factory, to produce two dollars' worth. There is a similar waste where the worker can increase his output by greater effort, care, attention, or initia-

WHAT IS WRONG WITH MONOPOLY?

tive in his work, but where he gets too little for his pains to make the effort worthwhile.

Perhaps the most important element in this kind of waste is in the worker's decision on how much work he wants to do. Whenever he has the freedom, he will choose to work up to the point where the pay he gets for an additional hour's work is just equal to the value to him of having an hour's more leisure, whether for doing some work at home or just for the enjoyment of rest and relaxation. What he would produce in the factory by an additional hour's work or by an additional effort may be worth $2, but if the pay is only $1, he will apply his time to leisure, or take it easier on the job, as long as the leisure or the ease is worth $1 to him. Everybody would gain even if he got only a *part* of the difference between his wage and the value of the marginal product. If, say, 40 cents over and above the $1 wage for the extra hour or effort induced him to do the extra work or make the extra effort, he would be better off (or he would not have agreed to provide the extra hour or effort) and yet there would be left over an additional 60 cents' worth of product for others to enjoy. Only if the wage throughout the entire economy is "correct"—i.e., *equal* to the value of the marginal product can we get the ideal division of time between work and leisure and between effort and relaxation.

What emerges from all this is that the harm done by monopoly (and/or monopsony) lies in *differential* restriction, and only in differential restriction. If there were exactly the same degree of restriction everywhere, no harm would be done to the efficiency of the economy. But since important areas in the economy are immune to restriction, or perfectly competitive by nature, any actual monopolies must be more monopolistic than these monopoly-free areas and therefore must entail *differential* restriction, and social waste.

With universal but equal degrees of monopoly and/or monopsony, there would indeed be higher prices and lower wages throughout the economy and therefore greater profits, but that is a matter of "fairness"—not of the "genuineness" or of "correctness" of prices and wages. Prices and wages would still be "correct." We might not like the resulting division of income between the different individuals in the society but that we must leave to Chapter XII on inequality of income and wealth.

CHAPTER VI

WHAT WOULD WE DO WITHOUT THE SPECULATOR?*

During the Spanish Civil War, when there was an agrarian revolution in Catalonia, I saw an excellent poster. The poster was of a farmer and his wife watching from the cottage door while their children went to play. The children were vegetables which the farmer had grown: a carrot, a tomato, a squash, and several others, gaily running and skipping toward the woods where there lurked an evil wolf, his greedy eyes fixed upon the children, his sharp teeth bared, and the saliva flowing freely from his mouth. The wolf was labeled the Catalonian equivalent of "speculator," the inscription on the poster was "Do not deliver your produce to the free market," and the Catalonian word for "produce" also seems to suggest "offspring." It was a beautiful poster, extremely well-done with attractive colors and the lesson was perfectly clear even to the illiterate. The speculator was the big bad wolf. The producers must not allow the speculator to get their crops, but should bring them to the state or to the co-operative, or to whatever organization it was that put out the poster.

The idea of the speculator as a wicked person appeals to many people for a number of reasons. The speculator seems to make money without giving any service in return. He does not produce; he merely buys and sells. He is a parasite who stands between the producer and the consumer, doing nothing except taking a rake-off for himself: a racketeer. Then the speculator takes chances, and we have a strong tradition about the immorality of gambling, even though it is frequently and widely violated. (Indeed, many kinds of gambling are perfectly proper and respectable if given another name, like dynamic enterprise.)

The notion that speculators or middlemen are unproductive may

* This chapter and the following one are adapted from an article "The Myth of the Parasitic Middleman," that appeared in *Commentary*, July, 1949.

be founded on time-honored distinctions between productive and unproductive activities. Actually the distinctions are misleading. The physiocrats in France—the intellectuals who sparked the French Revolution—developed what they called "natural laws" about economics. According to them, the man on the land was the only one who produced a *net product*. All others—industrial workers, professionals, public officials, and traders—only handle, or change the form of, the net product. But the physiocrats did not mean that traders and city workers are not useful. They were interested in something completely irrelevant to determining usefulness: they wanted to concentrate *taxation* on land, on the grounds that only land could be taxed without damaging the efficiency of the whole economic system.

Adam Smith made a different distinction between productive and unproductive labor, also irrelevant to our purposes. He distinguished between the production of physical goods, which could *directly* result in the accumulation of physical capital and thereby contribute to the growth of the wealth of nations, and the production of non-physical services which could not. And he took great pains to show that a great deal of "unproductive" labor was more useful than much "productive" labor.

In recent times certain circles of romantics and other circles of revolutionaries have glorified the manual worker, implying that all other people are useless and even pernicious. This is probably in part a healthy reaction to ancient beliefs that the so-called "lower classes" were inherently inferior and that manual labor was degrading. But the result of this reversal of the ancient myth was that managers and intellectuals were only grudgingly admitted to the realm of the socially useful, and then only on the grounds that their activities are a kind of work, something like that of the manual worker.

This relatively new myth of the superiority of manual labor, and many others that often go together with it, are of the same nature as nationalist prejudices. All virtues belong only to us and all vices belong to our enemies, who are inferior people anyhow. Such sentiments, so often utilized by national leaders against other nations during war and other times of stress, are also employed against the "bourgeoisie" by Marxist leaders of so-called proletarian revolutions. Hatred against the "bourgeoisie" is mobilized in exactly the same way as hatred has so often been mobilized against the foreigner or against the man with a different complexion. Karl Marx must have foreseen something of this, because he said, "Antisemitism is the socialism of the middle class," meaning, presumably, that the middle class was hating Jews instead of the capitalists whom they should be hating. But no good can come from any theory which puts all the evils of the world, and many imaginary ones, on the shoulders of a single "devil," whether it be the bourgeoisie or the Jews or the bicyclists.

A much more sensible reason for disliking the speculator is that he seems to raise prices; he makes things expensive in order to line his own pockets. An interesting experiment based on this idea took place in the Spanish Civil War. Everybody knew that at harvest time speculators came in and bought up crops to sell later at higher prices when food became scarce. When the speculators were chased away, to everyone's delight, wheat and bread were very cheap. There was great rejoicing. People who had not been able to afford white bread now bought it freely. It was even used for feeding cattle because it was cheaper than regular fodder. But soon the rejoicing faded. The bread and grain began to run low long before the next harvest. Then it was remembered that at this time of the year the speculators usually sold what they had bought at harvest time. But now there were no speculators and there was famine. It took this extreme suffering to teach the people that speculators do not merely buy, they also sell. If speculators can be blamed for causing prices to go up when they buy, they must also be credited with causing prices to go down (as well as with making the product available) when they sell. But instead of either blaming or praising speculators let us rather look at the important effects of their activities.

By a "speculator" I mean a man who buys something because he believes that the price is going to be higher later when he will sell at a profit. If his calculations (or his guesses) are right, he does make a profit. Sometimes he is wrong and he loses. He is not necessarily a large operator. The amount of buying or selling that he personally undertakes does not in itself influence prices; he merely tries to buy cheap and sell dear, and he can do this only by buying when things are cheap and selling when they are dear.

WITHOUT THE SPECULATOR?

Nevertheless, when speculators are buying anything, their competition does cause the price to rise. We cannot say that a price increase is good or bad *per se*; it is bad for those who are buying, but it is good for those who are selling, and we have to count the producers or sellers as citizens just as worthy as the consumers or buyers. But if we look a little more closely, we can compare the losses with the gains and reach some kind of impartial judgment. For this we must divide the sales into three parts.

First, there are sales made directly by producers to consumers. Here there is a gain and a loss which exactly cancel each other. The higher prices mean that the consumers pay more, but to exactly the same extent producers get more. There is no social loss, but a simple transfer from the consumer to the producer.

Second, there are sales which would have been made to consumers at the lower price but which at the higher price go to the speculators instead. Here there is a loss to the would-be consumers who find the price too high. But the producers, who get more from the speculators than the consumers are willing to pay, gain more than the would-be consumers lose.

Third, there are the extra sales which producers are induced to make because of the higher price. The extra sales are also made to speculators whose presence as purchasers is responsible for the higher price in the first place. On these sales there is a net benefit to producers without any loss at all to consumers.

The result of purchases by the speculators is a net gain to the rest of society.

Let me now illustrate how the gains exceed the losses. Suppose that in the absence of speculators 1,000 chairs would have been sold at a price of five dollars each; total sales would have been $5,000. The speculators arrive on the scene and because of their additional buying the price of chairs rises to six dollars. At six dollars the consumers buy only 800 chairs instead of 1,000. But the producers are so pleased at the higher price that they increase their output to 1,100 chairs, the 300 chairs not bought by consumers being taken up by the speculators.

Now we can look at the three parts of these sales. There are first of all the 800 chairs bought by the consumers. The consumers have lost a dollar on each chair because they have paid six dollars instead of five. On the other hand, the producers have gained a dollar on each chair. From a social point of view we may say that the gain cancels out the loss; taking producers together with consumers, they have neither gained nor lost.

Then there are the 200 chairs which the consumers decided not to buy because the price went up from five dollars to six dollars. The consumers would have been willing to pay varying amounts for the chairs. The difference between what they would have been willing to pay and the five dollars they would have been able to get them for if the speculators had not come into the picture, constitutes their loss. But the producers get six dollars per chair from speculators; they gain a whole dollar on each one, while the loss to the consumers is only a fraction of a dollar. The gain by the producers is greater than the loss to the consumers, so there is a net gain to producers and consumers taken together.

The third part consists of the sale to the speculators of the extra 100 units produced in response to the price increase. There is no loss to the consumers; they would not have bought any of the extra 100 chairs nor would the producers have manufactured them to sell at five dollars. But there is a gain to the producers of varying amounts up to a dollar each. They were not willing to supply more than 1,000 chairs at five dollars. If they had been they would have supplied more than 1,000 in the first place and the price would have been less than five dollars. But they are willing to supply 1,100 at six dollars. Therefore, the cost of production of the extra hundred chairs—the price at which they would have been just willing to supply them—varies between five and six dollars. The difference between this, the cost of production, and six dollars is their gain.

To summarize: in the first part the gain and the loss cancel out; in the second part the gain exceeds the loss; and in the third part there is pure gain. In total, therefore, there is a net gain to the producers and consumers taken together. Not (so far) counting the speculators, we may say that there is a net gain to society.

Now see what happens when the speculators *sell*. Suppose that in the absence of speculators 400 chairs would have been sold by producers at a price of eight dollars. The speculators' arriving and selling 300 units has the effect of reducing the price from eight to

WITHOUT THE SPECULATOR?

seven dollars. This reduction induces the consumers to increase purchases from 400 to 600 chairs, and it induces the producers to cut down their supply from 400 to 300. The other 300 are supplied by the speculators. Again we can divide the transactions into three parts.

First, there are the 300 chairs sold directly by the producers to the consumers. Here there is a gain by the consumers and a loss by the producers of one dollar per chair because the price is reduced from eight to seven dollars. The producers lose $300 and the consumers gain $300; taking producers and consumers together the two cancel each other out.

Second, there are the 100 chairs which the producers decide not to produce at the lower price, but which the consumers buy from the speculators instead. The producers lose an amount varying from zero to a dollar each chair by losing the profits they might have made from selling them at eight dollars. We know the loss comes to less than a dollar each, because the cost of production is more than seven dollars—otherwise the producers would not refuse to make them at seven dollars each. On the other hand, the consumers gain a whole dollar per unit when they buy at seven dollars what they would have bought at eight dollars. The gain to the consumers is greater than the loss to the producers on this 100. Here we have a net gain to the consumers and producers taken together.

The third part consists of the 200 additional chairs which the consumers buy because the price is lower. They buy these from the speculators; they would not have been supplied by the producers even at eight dollars. The producers therefore lose nothing in connection with these extra 200 chairs, but the consumers benefit from being able to buy at seven dollars each the 200 chairs for which they are willing to pay various amounts between seven and eight dollars. Taking all three parts together, we again see that there is a net gain to the producers and consumers taken together. They are benefitted first when the speculators buy and again when the speculators sell. As a result of the activity of the speculators there is a net gain to the rest of society (i.e., not counting the speculators).

To most people this argument at first seems a little too clever to be convincing. "Where," they ask, "does the benefit come from, since, after all, the speculators themselves are making a nice profit?"

This is a good question and deserves an answer. The benefit is derived from the *improvement in the use of resources*. Instead of a product being used wastefully because it is cheap, some of it is taken away by the speculators to be made available when it is more expensive—that is, when it is needed more. The speculator performs a function which is socially useful and he makes a profit by taking *a part* of the total benefit for himself.

What is perhaps even more surprising is that the rest of society, i.e., society exclusive of the speculators, benefits even when the speculators do the wrong thing—that is, when they sell at a lower price than that at which they buy—so that they have a loss instead of a profit. So far we have seen how the rest of society gains when the speculators buy, and how it also gains when the speculators sell. Nowhere have we discussed the speculators' profit. But if the speculators buy dear and sell cheap we cannot say that the benefits to society come out of an improvement in the use of resources. To the contrary, instead of improving the use of resources, speculators may have made it worse. But it is still true that *the rest* of society gains. Producers and consumers taken together still gain in exactly the same way as when the speculators are successful. They gain when the speculators buy and they gain once more when the speculators sell. But the gain is now at least in part at the expense of the speculators. There is a net social loss if the speculators lose more than the others gain. In this case the losses of the speculators must cover not only the benefits to the rest of society, but also the loss to society as a whole (including the speculators). The only people who should complain are the speculators (or their creditors, if the speculators are bankrupted).

What we have said about speculators who buy at one *time* and sell at another also applies to merchants who buy in one *place* and sell at another. They are also helping society use its resources efficiently, shifting resources from where they are needed less to where they are needed more. In this case, the activity is called commerce, or shipping or export and import, or simply *trade,* which hasn't such a bad name. But in the Soviet Union and its satellites this too is called "speculation" and is considered a capital crime. It was in the Soviet Union, nevertheless, that perhaps the clearest demonstration of the social usefulness of trade was provided when, in 1921, the economy seemed on the verge of collapse and Lenin permitted buying and selling—trading—under the New Economic Policy. Traders took things from places where they were not quite so scarce to other places where they were more scarce, and the result was that food and clothing were used more efficiently. Production was started up again, and all because traders were no longer threatened with severe punishment for "speculation." When the Soviet economy had been restored to a considerable degree, "speculation" was again prohibited and it still is, now perhaps more strongly than ever before.

In the western world, trading is not quite as improper a means of making money as speculation, perhaps because the benefits from moving goods in *space* are more easily seen than those from moving goods in *time*. Yet trading is hardly considered as noble an occupation as physical labor. But if we look closely at any kind of work, manual or otherwise, we shall find that it too is a form of trading. All work consists of moving things from one place to another, so that they might be used more efficiently; or, as one economist put it, all work consists of moving dirt from one place to another. No work consists of creating matter. It merely consists of rearranging matter, such as bringing coal from the bottom of the pit to the top, or moving it from there to factories and homes. All other work consists of similar, if less obvious, movements of matter. The weaver does nothing but rearrange the position of threads, the tailor does nothing but rearrange these threads so that they form the shape of a suit of clothes. The engineer does nothing but move a screw from one place to another and push it into its proper place. Even painting a picture has been described as simply putting the right colors in the right places on the canvas. All work consists of moving dirt or matter about, and it is useful work if it is the movement of materials from places where they are less useful to places where they are more useful.

Speculation may be condemned because the profits from speculation (or from trade) frequently seem excessive, and in some cases they are. The cure is nothing but *more* speculation. Profits are excessive because *not enough* has been moved from where the things are relatively plentiful to where they are relatively scarce. That is why there is still too great a price difference and too great a profit in speculation. If there were more speculators, the low prices would be bid up and the higher prices would be pushed down until the margin is so small that the speculator can just make a living. It may, indeed, be the disrepute itself which permits speculators to make excessive profits. Their bad name discourages some people from going into the business, so that those who do enter it can make large profits. The cure is to get rid of the disrepute. Speculation is desirable because it is in the best sense economical, as we saw in our example of cheap bread in Spain. When speculators were outlawed, the government and the cooperative societies had to become speculators themselves. They did just what the speculators had been doing although they did it less well, but only when they found themselves engaged in speculation did they recognize it as socially useful.

The competitive speculation, and the competitive trading, whose social usefulness we have been examining, must not be confused with socially harmful cornering of markets or establishment of monopolies. Such control over the market by combining with some and frightening others away, *restricts* the amount of speculative activity and the public must therefore be protected from such activities which unfortunately are sometimes also called "speculation." This leads to our next topic—the distinction between a business and a racket.

CHAPTER VII

THE MIDDLEMAN AND THE MIDDLE CLASS

The middleman is often attacked as nothing but a parasitic go-between. He is a trader who does not produce anything. He merely buys goods from the producer and sells them to the consumer at a profit. In times of inflation and of black markets and "gray" markets, he is also blamed for these phenomena.

Yet a moment's thought will serve to make one realize that the middlemen perform useful social functions. In the 1940's, for example, the "gray marketeers" broke through monopolistic practices and supplied buyers with vital materials such as steel, sorely needed to keep vital productive processes going, which could not be obtained by any other means. It is perhaps because we were uneasily aware of this that we changed the color from black to gray.

Yet even the middlemen themselves often plead guilty, deprecating their own social usefulness, admitting that they are parasites who not merely fail to do their fair share of work, but actually engage in socially harmful activities.

This apologetic attitude is quite uncalled for. We have seen that the work of the middleman, trader, or speculator consists in facilitating a socially desirable movement of things from where they are cheaper to where they are dearer, and that this means that things are moved from where they are needed less to where they are needed more.

One may object that there is no absolute certainty that the higher price really indicates any such thing; it may merely show that the buyers in the place to which the goods are moved have more money to spend. Thus the middleman might actually be taking goods away from poor people, who have a greater need for them, and selling them to rich people, who need them less. But the opposite is equally possible; the middleman may be taking goods from rich people and bringing them to poor people. After all, more goods are sold to poor people than to rich people—there are so many more poor people. In that case he is not only moving goods to where they are appreciated more—the basic benefit that results when goods are shifted between equally rich or equally poor consumers—but he is also moving goods from those who can spare them more easily to those who are in greater need of them.

Indeed, any general examination of the middleman's activities must begin by disregarding his shuttlings between rich and poor. Inequality of wealth and income is a separate problem, for which the middleman has no special responsibility. Properly understood, such inequality is merely a complicating factor in the middleman's activities. When he moves goods from poor to rich, the benefit is cut down; when the movement is in the other direction, the benefit is of course increased. Yet these variations cancel out on the whole, leaving the basic benefit of goods being shifted from where customers are willing to pay less to places where they are willing to pay more; and this still means that, given the existing distribution of income and wealth, they are being moved from where they are wanted less to where they are wanted more, from where they are less useful to where they are more useful. As we have seen in Chapter VI, this is all that is done by *any* productive work.

The Marxists have insisted that only labor is productive and that capital goods and land, although they are as essential to production as labor, are not. The same argument is sometimes applied to the activities of middlemen—that even if they help workers to be more productive, by guiding them to produce more useful things, they are not productive in themselves. Yet as a description of what actually happens, there is not the slightest difference between saying that land, capital or middlemen are productive and saying that they are not productive but they help labor to be more productive. If more capital or more land or more middlemen or traders or speculators are used with a given amount of labor, there will be a greater product, just as certainly as when more labor is applied. One could just as logically say that labor is not productive—it only helps land, capital and middlemen to be more productive!

The Marxists insist with such violence on labor's being the only "productive" force because they wish to harness the workers' sense

THE MIDDLE MAN AND THE MIDDLE CLASS

of property rights to the revolution: if the workers were the only "real" producers, then the product was by right completely theirs; if landlords, capitalists, or middlemen got anything at all out of the productive and distributive process, then they must in some hidden way be stealing it from its rightful owners. Many Marxists have been moved by this picture of capitalist pilfering to heights of proprietary passion that never could have come from a mere consideration of the desirability of social change. But however effective it may be for the purpose of kindling revolutionary fervor to claim a monopoly of "productiveness" for wage-labor, the distinction simply does not hold in any scientific analysis of how the economy actually works.

Sometimes the worker and the middleman are differentiated on the ground that one works for wages and the other for profit. Wages are then regarded as honorific, whereas profit is given a dishonorable connotation associated with the idea that it involves the exploitation of others. Part of the disesteem for profits comes from the ethical conception of a special selfishness in seeking profits—production should be "for use and not for profit." But why it is more selfish to work for profits than for wages is impossible to say. In both cases, personal gain is the incentive, and in neither is the motive pure patriotism or love of one's neighbors. Morally they are exactly on a par, and we are always driven back to the ultimate criterion of social usefulness.

This brings us back to the essential usefulness of the middleman, or speculator, in carrying goods (even though for profit) from where they are less urgently needed to where they are more urgently needed. In fact, a closer examination shows that the middleman can be *more* certain of his social usefulness than the "productive" worker.

The worker is normally engaged in turning a less useful thing, steel, into a more useful thing, an automobile. But there is no guarantee that the steel might not be needed for some other purpose even more urgently than for the automobile. The output of some alternative product, say locomotives, may be below what is socially desirable. In a capitalist society, this may be because a monopoly restricts output in order to keep up the price. In a socialist society, it may be the result of bad planning. In all such cases the automobile worker plays an innocent but none the less harmful role in turning a more useful thing—steel which is needed for locomotives—into a less useful thing—automobiles. Thus the worker can never be sure that what he is doing is really socially useful.

This is quite apart from the possibility that the worker might be participating in producing something to satisfy a rich man's whim instead of something to satisfy some poor man's urgent necessity. Such distortion in the use of resources is the result of inequality in income and wealth and is the exact parallel to the possibility that the middleman might be shifting resources from the poor to the rich. Just as in that case, this possibility must be balanced against the opposite possibility that the worker is engaged in producing for the poor when he might be producing for the rich. And again, like the middleman, the worker is not the one to blame for excessive inequalities of income and wealth. So long as labor and the other resources are being directed toward that product for which more money is being offered, the worker is engaged in turning less wanted goods into more wanted goods *relative to the given distribution of income and wealth*—just like the middleman. The point here is that because of a monopolistic or some other kind of restriction (for which he is not responsible) in another part of the economy, the worker may be engaged in moving things from where they are more useful to where they are less useful or making something more useful into something less useful.

The trader-speculator-middleman cannot damage the rest of society in this way. If he buys goods to sell them at a higher price elsewhere, there can be no doubt that they are wanted more in the place or at the time he carries them *to* than in the place or at the time he fetches them *from*. Thus, what he does is always socially useful; if it were not, he would be unable to make any profit. Furthermore, even if he should move things the *wrong* way, he will still be benefiting the *rest* of society. As we saw in Chapter VI, he will still be conferring a net benefit upon others both in the place where he buys and in the place where he sells, his losses covering not only these benefits, but absorbing any damage done to the economy as a whole by his error in moving goods the wrong way. The worker engaged in moving things the wrong way, just as he is not responsible, also does not pay the penalty. He gets his pay whether he is engaged usefully or harmfully.

This more certain productivity and usefulness of the middleman is attested to by his being able to survive in spite of all sorts of restrictions on his activities. The small traders, moving about from village to village or from town to town through the centuries knew only too well how multifold and ingenious these restrictions could be. Yet they always overcame them. Indeed, according to some, it was the scorned activities of such traders in the Middle Ages that made possible the beginnings of modern capitalism and the development of modern industry and modern standards of living.

The condemnation of such useful trading as "speculation," especially in the Soviet world, rests on a confusion between two different kinds of activity which unfortunately have been given the same name—speculation. The kind of trading discussed above may be called *competitive* speculation, to distinguish it from *monopolistic* speculation. Monopolistic speculation consists in *creating* scarcities. Sometimes this is done by *destroying* goods in order to sell the remainder at higher prices. But much more important than this destruction, since it occurs more frequently and on a larger scale, is the harm done in creating scarcity simply by limiting production. The greater part of the evil done by the monopolistic speculator thus lies not in what he takes out of the social product for himself, but in the part he destroys (or whose production he prevents) in order to be able to take a larger share of what remains. As a result, the rest of society is doubly impoverished—first by what the monopolist takes for himself and again by the reduction in the total output.

This kind of speculation cannot be carried on by the ordinary middleman. It involves an extensive control over productive resources, for without this control it is impossible to bring about artificial scarcity and the concomitant higher prices. The competitive speculator—the middleman—has no such powers. He cannot influence prices, for he is too small in relation to the total market; on the contrary, he must accept the prevailing prices. His activity can therefore only be the moving of goods from where he finds them cheap to where he finds them dear, to the net benefit of society (and to the net benefit of *the rest of* society even when the speculation moves them the wrong way and loses on the business).

It is sometimes argued that it cannot really be true that middlemen are useful or productive because it is clear that the economy could not live if everybody were a middleman and nobody engaged in direct production. But neither could the economy live if everybody became a coal miner or if everybody became a farmer.

It is also true that if there were a very good distribution of goods and services between different places and between different dates, and if this were brought about by a social authority without the use of middlemen, there would not be much for middlemen to do. But this does not mean that middlemen should be discouraged or restricted. It only means that if they could do so (which is the big question) the authorities should try to bring about such a perfect distribution that the middlemen would be unnecessary. A perfect distribution would show itself in balanced prices throughout the economy. The middlemen would then not be able to find any places where goods were relatively plentiful and cheap or where they were relatively scarce and dear.

To have such a perfect distribution of goods would of course be a good thing, quite apart from its effects in diminishing the need for middlemen and setting them free for other useful activities. But so long as middlemen can make a living by competitive speculation, this stands as proof of an insufficiently perfect distribution, and shows that they have not been rendered unnecessary.

The fact that middlemen would not be needed if distribution were perfect is no more significant than the fact that plumbers would not be needed if pipes never leaked. In actuality our water and gas pipes are not perfect and we do suffer from leaks. Yet no one supposes that the plumbing situation would be improved by decrying the usefulness of plumbers and imposing restrictions on their activity in repairing the leaks that do occur. If we don't want plumbers or middlemen, we must first find some way of improving the quality of piping or the efficiency of the distribution of goods so that plumbers or middlemen will find little to do and will be available for other jobs.

This can be applied more widely still. The man-hours needed for all sorts of operations are continually being reduced by increased efficiency and technological advances, and they would be reduced still further by the abolition of "featherbedding" practices. The ultimate in mechanization is presumably the complete elimination of the need for work altogether. Yet nobody has argued that this proves that workers are useless members of society today.

The question of the social role of the middleman has been complicated by a general tendency to take him as the prototype of the *middle class* and to confuse the two. This confusion might not be thought to matter very much because traders mostly *are* members of the middle class, occupying a place somewhere in the middle of the social hierarchy. It is, nevertheless, of importance to maintain a distinction between middlemen and the middle class, because the social usefulness of each is of quite a different nature. Middlemen are useful economically while the middle class is useful politically and sociologically.

The middle class includes not only the trader-middlemen-speculators, but also professional people, white-collar workers, highly skilled workers, and managers and specialists of various kinds— all who are neither at the top nor at the bottom of the hierarchy of wealth, status, and power, but somewhere in the middle. Useful as the middleman may be in improving the efficiency of the economy, and more certain though his usefulness may be in comparison with other groups of workers, the importance of the middle class for the maintenance of a good and free society is of a much higher order.

The middleman's function is to bring together the producer and the consumer. Those who do not understand his usefulness sometimes conceive of him as *separating* producers from consumers rather than joining them together, much as one might say that the mortar in a wall separates the bricks rather than joining them to each other. Actually, of course, what makes the wall stand is the way the mortar holds the bricks together. In the same way, the middle class, lying between the class below it and the class above it, performs the vital function of joining the classes together.

Although I have dealt here principally with the economics of the middleman, a similar analysis of the political and social roles of the middle class would seem to show that, by providing a continuous line of possible progress from the bottom to the top, a middle class tends to diminish the contrast between the extremes.

With the growth of the middle class, those who do not have a fair share in the privileges and advantages of society may have some hope for improvement and for an enlargement of such opportunities. This hope gives them the ground for interest in the general operation of the economy and in the organization of society. Moreover, they acquire a sense of responsibility for those parts of the social order which are of general utility and are not merely means for granting privileges to chosen minorities. They have a stake in the society—they have something more than their chains to lose—and this fact is of enormous importance; it means that their discontent can be harnessed to improve society rather than to destroy it, and that social changes are more likely to be of a kind which really benefit the great mass of the people.

A comparison of England, where there has been a strong middle class for centuries, with Germany, where the middle class was weak and had been ruined by the inflation, makes this point immediately clear. The Nazi movement was built on the mass support of those who had nothing to lose—the middle class who had been ruined and the unemployed who had lost hope. Where everybody sees opportunities for improvement and development, for himself, for his children, and for the members of society as a whole, the existing order does not appear wholly bad. There is less likelihood of blind revolutionary action, leaving the future entirely to unexamined and mystical benefits which are supposed to follow automatically from a complete destruction of the existing order. People are able to observe the agreement of experience with reason in showing that such blind action ultimately results in a situation worse than the one it replaces.

A strong and growing middle class assures the degree of social mobility and social responsibility that is necessary for real progress. True, the special weaknesses of the middle class played an important part in helping the demagogues of fascism and communism to hypnotize the hopelessly dispossessed with their deceptive slogans. Yet where there is a *strong* middle class, with social mobility, social responsibility, and the resulting social cohesion, there is always a much greater chance for an even wider distribution of social benefits without the sacrifice of freedom.

CHAPTER VIII

WHEN IS A BUSINESS A RACKET?

Almost every businessman, or anyone else, would be enraged at being called a racketeer. Yet when businessmen meet they often ask each other "Well, what is *your* racket?" and nobody's feelings are ruffled. The remark is not intended to suggest, even playfully, that they are malefactors or parasites who ought to be behind bars, but merely that their primary reason for being in business is the selfish one of making a profit, not the altruistic one of providing society with a needed service. In this sense all business is a "racket." But it is not more so than the activity of working men or professionals, who also perform their jobs for the equally selfish reason of being able to collect wages or salaries. On the other hand when we speak of a *real* racket, and of a racketeer, we think of someone who in some way harms society, quite apart from his making a living. We feel that he is doing something that he ought to be stopped from doing.

Critics of the capitalist or free enterprise system see in business something of actual racketeering—certainly they think ordinary business for profit should be stopped in the social interest. We might therefore look into what we mean by a "racket" and what it is that makes it bad. Perhaps the same evil is to be found in normal business, and the playful remark "what is your racket?" is an unconscious admission of something sinister!

We object to the racketeer in the first place for getting something for nothing when he collects "protection" money. "Protection" is the illegal collection of a tax by a private person; we think taxes should be collected only by the state in the social interest. Yet, strictly speaking, the collection of the tax by a racketeer does not in itself involve a social loss. It is merely the transfer of some profit from a firm to a racketeer; and there may be cases in which the firm has no better moral claim to the money than the gangster. The only social waste involved in this transfer is the energy and ingenuity of the racketeer that could be put to socially more useful ends, as well as the costs of the efforts of catching him and of keeping him in jail when he is caught.

Against this there is the socially useful function that may be performed by the racketeer in uncovering a possibility of a good tax. One important problem of society is to find taxes which interfere as little as possible with the economic mechanism. If the racketeer employs his ingenuity to find such possibilities, he is performing a social service. The government can take over the collection of the tax, thus putting the racketeer out of business, even if it does not put him in jail. Even the money that the racketeer collects before the government gets round to depriving him of his ill-gotten (or rather too easily gotten) gains, may be regarded as a worthwhile expense—like the truffles which the French farmer allows his pig to devour so as to encourage him to snuffle out more truffles. A good example is the gambling industry, which does not seem to be hampered at all by having to pay regular tribute to racketeers. It could therefore provide a convenient source of revenue to the government instead, and the racketeers could be eliminated altogether if the government collected all the tribute that the traffic could bear.

In most cases, however, the racketeer collecting tribute from an industry *does* damage the efficiency of the economy. But the nature of the damage is the same as that done by the perfectly legitimate collection of a tax by the government. The tribute or rake-off or "protection" money can be collected without affecting the use of resources only on those units of the output where the firm is making a profit greater than the amount of the tribute. Where the firm is making a profit of two dollars a unit and the collector demands a dollar out of this, there remains a dollar of net profit for the firm. The firm prefers to keep the remaining dollar rather than cut out the production so as to avoid paying the tribute. The economy works just as before, except that a part of the profit goes to the racketeer (or to the government). But where the profit on the unit is less than a dollar, the firm will stop producing the unit. This involves a real social loss. The gangster (or the tax collector) gets nothing, the victimized trader loses the profit he would have made, and the consumer loses to the extent that he was benefiting

WHEN IS A BUSINESS A RACKET?

from being able to buy something which is no longer available at a price he is willing to pay.

This brings us to the essence of the *social* harm done by the racketeer or the tax collector. He establishes a *barrier* between producers and consumers so as to be able to collect tribute on what passes through. The social damage is done not in connection with those goods and services which pay the tribute and pass the barrier, but in connection with those which do not yield enough profit to be able to pay the tribute and which therefore are prevented from passing through the barrier. It is this separation of the consumer from the producer—the *restriction* of production—that constitutes the social damage, rather than the robbery of the profits on those goods and services that get through.

Competitive business is just at the other extreme from this. Competitive business consists of *bringing together* the producer and the consumer. We have seen that this is especially true of the perfectly competitive speculator or middleman, even though he is often suspected of sinister doings. Competition facilitates the production and the distribution of the goods and services that the producers can provide for the consumers and perfectly competitive business not only brings together buyers and sellers, it brings them together to just the ideal degree.

In a perfectly competitive industry there is a tendency for abnormal profits to disappear because of the attraction of new competitors to a field. This continues until competition has reduced profits to normal—or no more than the "fair rate of return" needed to keep the business going. But such is not always the case. In certain circumstances very large profits can be made even though the industry is perfectly competitive, as in the example discussed in Chapter II. In a competitive economy a product like coal is sold at a price equal to the marginal cost—the cost of those units of coal that it is most expensive to produce. The price is therefore very much higher than the *average* cost and enormous incomes are earned by those mine owners who can produce a great part of their coal at much less than the marginal cost. Yet the price is not too high. The function of the price is to discourage the consumption to a degree that corresponds to the effort needed to produce an extra ton of coal in the least convenient and most expensive place.

All the coal which can be produced more cheaply is being produced already. Because an additional ton can be produced only at marginal cost, consumers should be discouraged from buying it. Thus large profits are not certain proof that an industry is being run like a "racket." They may be "rents" that emerge even though output is not being restricted below the optimum.

But what about the monopolistic business? The monopolist knows that the volume of his business influences the market, affecting the price at which he buys or sells. It pays him to restrict his buying and selling because this lowers the price at which he can buy or raises the price at which he can sell. Consequently he does *not* produce the ideal volume where the selling price equals the marginal cost. If he should by accident reach it, he would cut back on his volume because he gains more from the larger profit per unit than he loses from the reduction in volume.

The monopolist hurts the efficiency of the economy by restricting output just as the racketeer does. Yet the monopolist is no more likely than the perfectly competitive businessman to refer to his business as a racket, and he would be just as incensed as the perfectly competitive businessman at the suggestion that he was a racketeer. Although he admits to being in business mainly to make money for himself (or for his pet charitable organizations), he will insist he is doing what is socially useful, and perhaps even essential, for the health, comfort, or security of his fellow citizens. Like the competitive speculator or producer or trader, he too is engaged in moving things from where they are wanted less to where they are wanted more. What he is doing is as useful as what is done by his competitive colleague who is perhaps only more competed against than positively competitive.

There is no reason for supposing that the monopolist is (in general) a more selfish person than the competitive businessman—both are out for maximum profits—nor is he likely to be less idealistic in the way he spends his earnings. Indeed, to the degree that he earns more, and this is usually, though not necessarily, the case, he is likely to be more idealistic and more altruistic in his spending. He can more easily afford it.

The difference between the monopolist and the racketeer, which may be responsible for the monopolist's good conscience, is that the social evil is to be found in what the monopolist *does not do,*

WHEN IS A BUSINESS A RACKET?

while it is to be found in what the racketeer *does do*. The racketeer goes about reducing output below the social optimum and what he does results only in harm to society. The monopolist does *good* to society in the economic activities he undertakes. The only thing wrong is that he does not do enough of it. Nevertheless the damage done to the economy is the same.

Just as large profits are no proof of the existence of a racket or a monopoly, so the *absence* of large profits is no surety of their absence. Monopoly can harm society even when profits are low. Consider the retailing of candy, for example. Each candy store has a special market in the many people who live nearby or happen to walk past it. Many passers-by will patronize the candy store, even if they can get the same candy for less at some other place. This means that the owner of the candy store is not operating under conditions of perfect competition. He monopolizes his small market, or at least part of it. If he charges a higher price, he does not lose all his customers to other candy stores, nor is he swamped by customers if he charges a lower price. And so it pays him to make his price higher than the marginal cost of providing the customer with an extra pound of candy. He sells less but he makes a larger total profit because his sales are not greatly reduced. Yet because each candy store's market is small, the large profit per pound of candy yields only a small return on the investment—no more, in fact, than what is necessary to make it worthwhile to carry on the business. This is no accident; it is the result of more people getting into the candy store business as long as there are *any* extra profits, thus reducing the market for each store until the extra profit has disappeared.

Although there is no large profit in running these monopolistic candy stores, damage is still done to society. The public must pay a higher price for candy. Nobody gains from the higher price, which is all wasted on the inefficiency of having too many stores, each selling too little. The people running such monopolistic businesses (gas stations are another example) always complain of too much competition. What they mean is that there are too many monopolists in the business, splitting up the market into smaller sub-markets and eliminating the profits that could have arisen from the higher prices.

Another kind of monopoly, which also damages the economy by

reducing output below the social optimum, is the restriction of entry into an industry or occupation which otherwise might be perfectly competitive. This is in one way just the opposite of the candy retailing industry where the profits were dissipated because too many entered the industry. Here it is the restriction of entry that makes it possible for larger incomes to be earned and for larger profits to be made.

Sometimes entry in an industry is kept down by real racketeers threatening arson and murder. Less monstrous ways of keeping competition away, such as high entrance or license fees paid to respectable organizations that nobody would call rackets, or requirements of unnecessary years of apprenticeship or of underpaid "internships," are sometimes also frowned upon as anti-social. But limitations on entry into an industry can be imposed in other ways which at first glance seem socially harmless; they are frequently applied with excellent intentions. An agreement among the people in any occupation to keep up the price which they charge for a product or service does not look like a restriction on people going into that occupation, but the results are the same. The higher the price of a product, the less the consumers can buy and the fewer the people who can find employment. Similarly, workers who would be shocked at the idea of openly preventing others from entering their occupation may feel justified in urging their union to secure an increase in wages and to maintain a system of seniority. Nobody is directly told to keep out, but it is made difficult for anybody to get in. The higher wage means higher cost and less demand for the services and consequently fewer jobs. The seniority rules deny jobs to newcomers in favor of those who have been in for a time.

The demand for higher wages in low-wage areas, whether by law or by national labor organizations, such as an insistence that the wages in the South be as high as they are in the North, can have similar unfortunate results. Such proposals are supported by people who would shudder at the thought that they were discriminating against or in any way hurting the laborers in the South. But the effect is that many laborers in the South are unable to find employment. The greater supply of labor and the lesser availability of capital there means that workers can be employed only at lower wages. Lower wages would indeed mean larger profits for industry, but lower wages and higher profits are just what would bring about the cure. More northern capital would be drawn to the South to take advantage of the larger profits and more southern labor would be induced to move to the North to enjoy the higher wages. The fixing of wages at a high level in the South prevents the desirable adjustment from taking place in reducing the incentive for capital to move to the South, and it tempts labor to stay in the South in order to gamble on landing one of the scarce high-paid jobs.

It is hard to say exactly whether anyone benefits from such a wage policy, which is often claimed to be in the interests of the southern workers. But it is difficult to make a convincing case for this claim if the alleged beneficiaries try to avoid the supposed benefit—e.g., if some southern workers would prefer to work for a lower wage rather than stay unemployed. Perhaps the damage done all around is so great that nobody benefits; but it is possible that northern workers gain in greater employment and higher pay because the workers staying in the South do not enter into direct competition with them.

What monopolies and socially harmful rackets have in common is the restriction of output below the social optimum, but there is a more direct connection between them. The activity of the monopolist can be considered as consisting of two parts. One is the provision of the useful service, which is good; and the other is the restriction of output.

Reduction of output and restriction of entry is frequently taken over by the racketeer proper—especially where it is difficult for the members of the industry to get together themselves. The gangster can then use violence or the threat of violence to organize the industry, trade union, or industry via the union, establishing a monopoly profitable enough to be able to pay the racketeer's fee. This is why rackets are hard to eliminate. They perform a service that is of benefit to the organization even though it imposes much greater losses on the community as a whole.

Borderline cases of course exist, as when a city trade union boycotts electrical goods or plumbing fixtures produced outside the city by workers who are getting less than the city union rates of pay. It is hard for a trade union leader who organizes such a boycott to understand why anyone should object and call him a racketeer, especially if he is not doing this for his personal gain but as an honest service to the members of his union, and especially if he notices that the federal government does just this when it "protects" domestic industry from "unfair" competition by foreign imports.

From this example it might appear that whether a particular activity constitutes a racket may merely be a legal question of whether the activity is authorized or prohibited by law—or simply a question as to what we consider *morally* permissible. But we are concerned here only with the question of when business serves or harms the public, and the public is harmed by monopolistic restrictions of output.

The social usefulness of business activities has been questioned in other ways. A business may be creating a need in order to make a profit in satisfying it. A great deal of money is spent, for example, in making people afraid of smelling like human beings. It is then possible to sell them chemicals which will reduce the human smell. Is this a socially useful activity or a racket?

Here, too, negative and positive elements can be distinguished. Once the fear of or dislike for the human smell exists, the manufacture and sale of the cure for it serves a human want just like any other, and the activity of providing that satisfaction serves to make people happier, just like any other service that satisfies a natural need. But the creation of the need is a *disservice*. After the victims have spent their money in satisfying their new want they are no better off than they were before the want was created. Useful production, e.g., by reducing hunger or providing shelter and warmth, always destroys or eliminates a want by satisfying it. Just as the destruction of wants is the mark of positive production so the creation of wants is *negative production* or *anti-production*.

Some critics of capitalism would discount the preferences of the public as guides to what should be produced, not only in cases like the antisocial manufacture of wants just discussed, but in general. They claim that consumers' preferences are only the result of capitalist conditioning and that it would be best to produce instead the things that experts know are good for people. One wonders where one would find experts who are not conditioned by the

WHEN IS A BUSINESS A RACKET?

society in which they live. But more important is the way this argument fails to make the crucial distinction between *creating* harmful or unnecessary wants, which is bad, and *providing* people with what they happen to want, which is good, no matter how the want came into existence, if we accept the democratic principle that each man is the best authority on what he himself wants.

This criticism of capitalism betrays an anti-democratic or totalitarian point of view which can justify the disregard, not only of the preferences of consumers, but of the views of political opponents who may be overridden or liquidated once their views are outlawed as not "genuine." The moral is not that consumers' preferences should be disregarded, but that the use of advertising for the creation of new wants should be prohibited as antisocial antiproduction—even if not as pernicious as the creation of positively harmful wants like a craving for narcotics or cigarettes.

Another type of business activity that is properly called a racket is the production of goods that defraud the buyer by not doing what they are supposed to do. But here too one should distinguish between the harmful part of the activity that consists of misleading the public and the positive part which consists of providing the goods that the public has been made to want, if one is not to condemn wrongly. Some time ago the papers reported someone cutting up bars of soap and selling each slice for $1.50 as a compound for cleaning automobile windshields. This was denounced a racket, and for lack of a more honest charge he was jailed for "vagrancy." Yet he was not doing any harm to anybody. His customers benefited. Their windshields were cleaner and he might even have prevented some automobile accidents. He was able to make a large profit only because not enough others had thought of competing with him and pushing the price down closer to the costs. It is true that if he had published his recipe he would have made fewer sales, but we do not insist all businesses publish their trade secrets. On the contrary we punish industrial espionage. And why should we expect him more than anyone else to engage in a crusade to tell people to wash their windshields and show them it can be done with ordinary soap? The only thing really wrong was that he had not organized his business on a large enough scale to be considered respectable and that his industry was insufficiently competitive so that there was a temporary monopoly. This would be diminished when others entered the trade and would be completely eliminated when the competition widened to include every one who had some soap in the kitchen.

Nor are all of the activities that are called rackets socially harmful. But sometimes the use of illegal force to *increase* competition is called a racket. Men who want to evade regulations, the main function of which is to restrict competition, sometimes resort to "racketeers," like the union leader who takes a bribe for permitting the use of non-union materials, or a building inspector who takes a bribe for disregarding unreasonable or out-dated building regulations. The racketeer in such cases is helping to benefit the public at large, although he is betraying his trust to the restrictive monopoly. Such beneficial rackets are, however, exceptional and certainly society would gain from the elimination of rackets of every kind.

The racket element in business, however, is peripheral. It must constitute a relatively small part of the activity of business or modern society could not have been as successful as it has been in raising the standards of living to the present high level.

CHAPTER IX

ECONOMIC DEMOCRACY
(OR, THE MARKET AND THE BALLOT)

Many critics of democratic capitalist societies claim that political democracy is not enough—that it needs to be supplemented by economic democracy. Political democracy gives each man an equal vote concerning the conduct of government; economic democracy would give each person the same amount of power concerning the production, distribution, and consumption of wealth or income. All men would then be equal economically as well as politically. There would be neither rich nor poor, just as there would be neither powerful nor weak, neither oppressors nor oppressed.

This view of "economic democracy" is very closely related to the idea of economic equality. The absence of economic democracy in this sense is attributed to private property and private enterprise. The way to achieve economic democracy therefore seems to be to abolish private property and private enterprise.

There is a fundamental confusion in such a lumping together of economic democracy, economic equality and the abolition of private enterprise and private property. It would be quite possible to eliminate all private property and all private enterprise without getting any of the benefits hoped for by those who desire economic as well as political democracy—witness Soviet Russia and Nazi Germany where limitations in varying degrees of the rights of private property and private enterprise did not prevent unprecedented oppression.

We might better ask, "What do we fundamentally mean by democracy?" Fundamentally we mean respect for the individual—a willingness to recognize individual desires and preferences and a readiness to satisfy them except where this would interfere even more with the desires and preferences of other individuals.

Sometimes democracy is equated with majority rule. But rule by the majority, while doubtless preferable to rule by the minority, does not touch the essence. It is not democracy if a majority wantonly oppresses a minority any more than if a minority oppresses a majority. It is not democracy if a majority, for example, forces a minority to adopt and practice the majority's religion. On occasion, the absolute overruling of a minority by a majority cannot be avoided; but genuine democracy is much more than majority rule. It implies fairness, reasonableness, consideration of the sentiments and interests of special groups, and taking into account not merely the numbers of people with different preferences, but the degree to which the issues matter to different people. Minorities should not be repressed unless the only alternative is as severe a repression of the majority. Fortunately, it is rarely necessary to choose between two such stark alternatives.

These views of democracy are pretty widely held in our country. Most Americans believe, for instance, that proportional representation, whatever other shortcomings it may have, is democratic, in that it assures minorities that they will not be under-represented in legislative assemblies even if their votes are so spread that they have majorities in very few constituencies and possibly in none. We also believe it democratic, when a group of people are engaged in a common enterprise, for those who put more money or effort into it than others to have a larger number of votes in its management. (There may arise the question of whether the people who put more into an enterprise did so only because they were richer rather than more interested, and whether they were justly entitled to be richer in the first place. But let us ignore that problem for the moment. It is once more the question of justification for inequality of income or wealth which is coming up in Chapter XII.) In cases of this kind we find not the simple absolute majority rule of "one man one vote," but a system by which the degree of concern that the party has in the undertaking is given due weight in the number of votes he can cast. The most extreme form of unequal voting is to be found in the limiting case where the issues are of concern only for one person. We agree that a person has the right to do whatever he wants with his own spare time, or in his own home, or with his own property, as long as no one else is harmed. This is equivalent to giving him *all* of the votes on such activities and none to anyone else. Yet we see nothing undemocratic in such free-

ECONOMIC DEMOCRACY

dom of the individual. On the contrary we would maintain that interfering with his freedom would be undemocratic.

A number of people, concentrating on this aspect of democracy and dissatisfied with the ways in which modern complex civilization interferes with individuality and privacy, have built for themselves an imaginary golden age in the past in which everybody produced everything he needed or wanted all by himself in his own house or garden. He did not depend on anybody for anything and could not be interfered with by anybody. Like the Jolly Miller he could sing "I care for nobody no not I / And nobody cares for me." He could produce one thing, if he preferred it, or he could produce something else instead. He could work as long as he liked or as little as he liked and nobody cared. He could devote himself to the accumulation of material things or he could concentrate his attention on spiritual matters, and again nobody could gainsay or interfere with him. This is called the Distributist Ideal.

Whether or not anything approaching this ever happened in the past, it seems quite clear that it could not be done on a large scale today. The amount of production necessary not only to maintain modern standards of living but just to keep alive the present large population on our planet is impossible except by mass industrial production. If we were to give everybody a piece of land on which he had to produce by himself everything that he needed, everybody would starve to death. But we do have a mechanism by which the same result can be achieved, and to a certain extent is achieved, without giving up the efficiency of modern mass production. The instrument which does this is of course the *market*.

The market can be considered as an instrument for distributing goods among different people *democratically,* i.e., in accordance with their individual preferences as shown by their willingness to vote for them by spending money on them. If the goods were distributed in any other way, e.g., by a non-democratic authoritarian rationing technique, we would have an inferior distribution of goods; it would not be possible for each person's preference to be taken into consideration by whoever was in charge of the distribution.

Non-market distribution could be very much improved upon if persons were free to barter their rations with each other. Every such exchange could only benefit the people concerned, because if either party to an exchange were not benefited he would simply refuse to participate. But for each person to look for somebody else who has the things he wants to get and who happens to want what he has to give, would take up so much time that it would be extremely wasteful and inefficient.

The market, by placing the goods conveniently in stores and by providing the consumer with some money with which he can directly buy what he wants, gives us immediately the same results which could be obtained in a barter economy only after endless searching and exchanging and re-exchanging.

In doing this the market performs the democratic task of bringing about a distribution or allocation of goods that takes into consideration the preferences of all the individuals as between the different goods. It is as if it allowed each individual to vote, with dollars, as to which of the available goods and services he wanted to have, and then *fulfilled all the election promises*—giving him the things he voted for. The market also permits each individual to vote in different degrees for different items, and in different degrees for additional amounts, in a way which is much beyond the possibilities of the ballot as a modern skyscraper is beyond a simple mud hut.

But this is only the first of the results brought about by the market as a kind of super-ballot system for achieving economic democracy. This result is what was described in Chapter II as the function of "genuine" prices. But if the "genuine" prices are also "correct" prices, as described in Chapter III, the market brings about all the benefits of the imaginary ideal distributist society of self-sufficient households, because the "correct" prices constitute guides directing those things to be produced which consumers prefer. If there is an increase in the demand for any item, it yields an extra profit. Producers, seeking this profit, expand output, thereby adjusting production to demand. In this way the consumer is able to vote effectively for the *production* of the different things he wants. He votes when he puts down his dollars, and the things he votes for get produced and delivered to him.

Furthermore, the economic "voter" is not left—as in political balloting—to choose between two or three candidates, neither of

ECONOMIC DEMOCRACY

whom may appeal to him very much; there are literally millions of things on which he can vote and on which he can vote for in differing *degrees* and get them in different *amounts*. Whether he wants more clothing or more housing or more holiday travel; whether he wants more underwear or more ties or socks, or whether he wants cotton or wool or nylon; whether he wants some of these for some items and some for others, whether he wants a particular kind of weave in the wool or nylon or another kind, or different proportions or combinations of mixtures between them, he can vote for these and get them to the *degrees* and in the *quantities* that he chooses. This is called *consumers' sovereignty*, and forms an essential part of economic democracy.

The "correct" prices and wages also lead to the ideal choice by workers, i.e., the perfectly free and democratic choice, as to how hard or how long to work—just as in the ideal distributist society. If the wage is a "genuine" wage, i.e., if the worker has a genuine opportunity to work as much or as little as he wants to at the wage, he will work another hour or make an extra effort only as long as he prefers the pay to the leisure or the ease that he has to give up in order to get it. This, however, does not give us the ideal degree of work or effort unless the wage is also "correct," i.e., unless the wage is equal to the value of the marginal or extra product resulting from the extra work in hours or in effort.

If the wage is less than the value of the marginal product, the worker will do less than the most desirable amount of work. He will stop at a point where the extra product is still worth more than the extra effort that would be needed to produce it. This is wasteful underproduction, and is the result of the worker not getting all that he is voting for by his expenditure of working time or effort. If the wage is greater than the value of the marginal product, the worker will do too much work. He will work up to a point where the extra product is worth *less* than the extra effort by as much as its value is less than the pay. With "correct" prices and wages, both of these forms of waste are avoided.

From another point of view this may be seen to maximize *freedom*. If the wage is just equal to the value of the marginal product, the rest of society is quite indifferent as to whether he works harder or the opposite. If he makes the extra effort, his extra pay takes away from the total product just as much as his effort adds to it, so that there is just as much left over for others as before. If he decides to take it easy, the reduction in his pay just cancels the reduction in total output and there is again just as much left over for others as before. He is not doing a favor or a disfavor to others by working harder or by working less; nobody is obligated to anybody—just as in the distributist ideal—so that, just as in the case of the Jolly Miller, there would be no social pressure on the individual to work harder (or the opposite). That is the essence of independence and freedom.

It might seem that consumers' sovereignty applies only to a small part of our economy, since most goods are bought not by consumers but by firms. But the preference of the consumer works itself way back through all the things which are sold by firm to firm. If at the current prices the consumer prefers nylon to woolen socks, the retailer and the wholesaler will demand nylon socks, and the sock manufacturers will demand nylon. This demand will be reflected in the nylon manufacturer's demand for chemicals, and so on through no matter how many steps in the enormous complexity of our economy.

But there are a number of other conditions which must be satisfied if we are to reach true economic democracy with consumers' sovereignty. These conditions have by no means yet been fully satisfied in modern societies, although they have been sufficiently met to provide a higher standard of living and greater opportunities for its members than was ever possible before.

First, there must be a free market in which people can buy or sell what they want without any restrictions and in which the prices are those that clear the market. Otherwise, they cannot freely exercise their dollar votes.

Second, there must be no restrictions, open or hidden, on anybody's going into any occupation nor may there be any special privilege. Equality of opportunity is basic to economic or any other kind of democracy. Without equality of opportunity some people cannot freely earn the dollars with which to vote and with the resulting "incorrect" prices, there is not the correct delivery of the items voted for. If people are not able to get certain jobs because they lack experience and then cannot get experience because they cannot get the jobs, they are being effectively kept out. The restriction may benefit those who are in, but it interferes with true economic democracy. The same thing is true if tradition or prejudice creates obstacles for a particular race or sex, or if it takes a lot of money or political and family connections for a person to acquire a certain skill. In modern democracies, more and more such restrictions have been removed by way of subsidized education, educational loans and scholarships, although it is by no means true that the poor man has just the same opportunities as a rich or well-connected person.

Third, there must be no monopolistic restriction of the output of any product in order to keep up its price, or any monopsonistic restriction in the input of any factor of production in order to keep its price down. As was shown in Chapters III and IV this causes a departure from "correct" prices and distorts the voting power of the dollars.

Fourth, taxes must not interfere too much with the "correct" prices and thus with the efficiency of the economy. Taxes tend to interfere with the efficiency of the economy by raising prices relatively to marginal cost and thereby above the "correct" level, but different taxes do so in different ways and some interfere very little.

A fifth condition essential to any reasonable approximation to the ideal of economic democracy is that there should be no depression or inflation—most particularly, no depression. A democracy must maintain the dignity of every individual, including that of the worker. He is now given considerable protection in our country by social legislation and by labor organizations, but there is nothing which can give him so much dignity as the knowledge that if he is not being treated well he can leave his job and get another one without much difficulty. His employer is then not doing him a particular favor by employing him, any more than he is doing his employer a favor by working for him.

The ability of a worker to leave his job easily is not the same thing as the right to strike. A decision to strike is made not by the individual worker but by a union, and the degree to which the opinions of the members of the union influences the decision, varies from union to union. The union can increase the dignity of the individual by protecting him from unfair treatment by his employers, but the union can also be an organ of oppression. By far the most effective protection of a worker against unfair treatment by his employer is his ability to quit and quickly get another good job. This he cannot do if there is a depression.

From what I have said so far it might seem that we would never need to make use of the political ballot, the market being so enormously superior. But this is not so. The political ballot is necessary to establish general rules which must be observed by everybody. If it is decided, for example, that a market system should exist, in which case it would have to apply to everybody, or that the nation needs an army that would presumably defend everybody, a minority that disagrees will have to be overruled—unless they come to outnumber the others on this matter (in which case, of course, they become the majority) or if they feel so much more strongly about the issue than the majority that the majority thinks it better to give way.

Such a decision is by nature a *public* decision, not a *private* one. A private decision is a decision by a man to do something which does not affect others. If I decide to work harder and then use the proceeds to buy more goods, there is just as much left for everybody else, as we have seen above. This is what makes my decision a private decision.

The market can in fact be correctly described as an instrument for making decisions private which would otherwise be public. (There are of course other decisions that are private in any case, like whether I will read or sleep this evening.) The "correct" price or wage is precisely the price or wage which leaves others unaffected by anyone's decision to work more or work less or to buy more or buy less of any item. That is what makes the decision private. An "incorrect" price or wage does not do this. When I decide to buy more at an "incorrect" price or to work more at an "incorrect" wage, there is either more left or less left for others. Where the price or wage can be made "correct" this is remedied and the decision is made private.

The distinction between private and public decisions turns out to be the same as the distinction between economic and political matters. If it is possible, by using devices such as private property and the market, to enable those who want something to get it

ECONOMIC DEMOCRACY

without interfering with others, then the decision can be made a *private* one. In the interests of freedom it is desirable to do this wherever possible. And every time we succeed in doing this, we shift something from politics into economics. Economics can use the superior system of the super-ballot which we call the market, not because economists are smarter than political scientists, but because wherever anybody discovers or invents a method of doing this so that the issue can be handled by the market—and he may be a lawyer or an engineer, a mathematician or even a political scientist—the economists grab it and say it is part of their realm. It stops being politics and becomes economics.

The distinction between private and public, between economic and political, breaks down where people can complain that they *do* care what other people do privately in their own homes or with their own spare time. But such complaints do not fit in with a free society, even if they are made by a very large majority. In a truly free society you must be allowed to do anything you like as long as it does not interfere with anything anyone else wants to do.

CHAPTER X

HOW THE MONEY GOES ROUND—PROSPERITY, DEPRESSION, INFLATION

So far we have looked mainly at the positive side of our economic system; we have seen how prices and wages that are both "genuine" and "correct" can make production for profit a most efficient form of production for use. We have, indeed, referred to a number of imperfections or limitations, but that was only in order to combat certain exaggerations, to point out that we have done pretty well on the whole in spite of these, or to postpone discussion of the flaws to a later chapter.

One limitation we have mentioned several times is that every dollar counts as much as every other dollar in its influence on the economic mechanism. Quite unimportant luxuries for the rich (and even for their pets) may have precedence over important needs of the poor because there is a greater demand for the former in dollars. The examination of the degree to which adjustments can or should be made for this must be left to Chapter XII.

Another limitation we have discussed is the departure from the ideal whenever there is any restriction of activity in some part of the economic system—by open or hidden barriers to entry to various fields of economic activity or by imperfection of competition, i.e., a monopolist restricting output in order to obtain a higher price or a "monopsonist" buying less in order to buy cheaper. As a result, the displaced resources can only be used to produce items that are in less urgent demand.

Yet another weakness is a bias in the system against "social goods" which benefit the public generally rather than, or in addition to, particular individuals separately. Such products are national defense, police services, sanitary facilities, and non-technical education. In the case of such "social goods," an individual purchaser working through the market will either not demand the product at all or will buy less than is socially desirable. He will normally want to pay only for the benefit that he enjoys himself and not for the benefit that accrues to others. Or he will wait for somebody else to buy the product or service when he will benefit without paying anything. "Social goods" will be adequately provided only in response to *social purchase* by combinations of the beneficiaries in the neighborhood, the city, the state or the nation; and agreement on such combinations are not easy. Perhaps the most important instance of this at the present time is the difficulty of purchasing security from mass destruction in a thermonuclear war. Such security is a product that can be bought only by the combination of the beneficiaries in an international organization that would constitute a world government.

The particular problem to which this chapter is devoted arises from the fact that the decisions governing how much should be produced of any item at the same time determines how many jobs will be provided in producing the item. It follows immediately that the total number of jobs provided in the whole economy, being the sum of the jobs provided by all the separate industries, is a by-product of the separate decisions as to how much to produce of the separate items. If this total is just right it will give employment to all the people who would like to work, and we have prosperity. But it may be *too much* and it may be *too little*.

If total spending is too little we have depression. Profits are low, business is bad, and there are too few jobs. And the degree of unemployment and of depression is related to the degree to which total spending is too little. There is too much total spending when people try to buy more goods than can be made even if everybody who wants to work is employed. Goods and labor then become scarce, prices and wages rise, and we have inflation, which, as we know, leads to injustice, to inefficiency, and to the disorganization of the economy.

It is natural for the businessman to believe that the cause of unemployment is that wages are too high, and that the cure for it is to cut the wage. He knows from experience that if he could pay lower wages his costs would be lower, he would be able not only to make more profit but to sell more goods (even if it meant cutting the price somewhat) and to employ more workers.* He then goes

---

* It is just as natural for him to believe the converse, namely, that the cause of inflation is that wages are too low, because he knows that if he had to pay higher wages he would have to raise his prices and that this would check any excess demand for his product. But he does not stress this—in part because

on to declare that what is true for every business must be true for all businesses taken together. But this is just where he goes wrong. He has stopped talking about his own business, where he knows what he is talking about, and has started talking about "everybody's business" where things are different. His experience is valid only for a particular firm, industry or region. It is not applicable to the problem of inflation or depression in the whole economy. In his business an excess demand *would* automatically be cured by a moderate increase in prices or wages and a deficiency of demand *would* be cured by a moderate cut in prices and wages. But *there is no satisfactory automatic mechanism for equalizing the supply and demand for jobs in the economy as a whole.*

Right at the beginning, in Chapter I, we met the young man who could not see anything *right* about the competitive capitalist system. His counterpart is the man who has been so hypnotized by the positive workings of the pure mechanism (which we have been stressing so far in this book) that he has fallen into the opposite error of not being able to see anything *wrong* about the competitive capitalist system. A brilliant example of this is provided by Henry Hazlitt's "Economics in One Lesson,"* where Hazlitt provides an excellent description of the ideal working of the price mechanism if not disrupted by foolish or partisan policy. But in assuming that full employment without inflation is somehow being maintained, he fails to notice the absence of any satisfactory machinery for achieving this objective or even to recognize the possibility of the existence of a problem in this connection. This blind spot is the chief reason for and the main content of his more recent book, "The Failure of the 'New Economics.' "†

What our businessman, and Mr. Hazlitt, fail to see is the difference between a particular firm, region or industry and the economy as a whole—the difference that makes false for the economy as a whole what is true for each part of it.

It is true of any firm, industry or region—as we saw in some detail

---

he encounters nothing like the same resistance to raising wages as he does when he attempts to reduce them—but even more because he has no serious objection, as a rule, to raising his price *without* raising wages, and this is just as effective in curing any excess demand for his product.

* New York, Harper, 1946.
† Princeton, Van Nostrand, 1959.

in Chapter IV—that if the wage rose whenever there were more vacancies than applicants for jobs, and the wage fell when it was the other way around, the wage would come to rest only when the number of men looking for jobs was just equal to the number of jobs looking for men, supply equal to demand, the market cleared and the wage "genuine." But this works primarily, as was emphasized in Chapter IV, because the wage is raised or lowered *only in that firm, region or industry*. What is essential is that it should be a change *relatively* to the rest of the economy. The mechanism does not work if the wage is changed in the economy as a whole (in response to a *general* inflation or depression in the economy as a whole) because in that case there is no *relative* change—there are no other wages relatively to which the wage could have changed.

The main reason why an increase in wages in our particular business or industry or region cures an excess demand for labor are (1) we lose customers because we have to raise our prices, (2) we shift from using labor to using machinery and intermediate products, and (3) labor moves into our industry from outside. But if wages are raised throughout the economy (in response to an inflation throughout the economy) there is no reason why any of these shifts should occur; (1) raising our price does not drive customers away—the other things they can buy have also become more expensive, (2) we do not substitute machinery and materials for labor—machinery and other materials have not become any cheaper relatively to wages because their prices have risen with the rise in the wages paid in making them, and (3) workers do not move into our region—wages have also gone up where they are now.

Similarly, if there is a general depression, a wage cut in our firm, industry or region will not enable us to induce customers to switch to us if wages elsewhere, including those paid by all our competitors, have been cut to the same degree and for the same reason; a wage cut will not induce us to substitute labor for machinery if the machinery has also fallen in price; and a wage cut will not cause our workers to move elsewhere if wages have been cut elsewhere too.

But faith in the system having some automatic cure for depression or inflation is not easily destroyed. The believer now comes back with a new and different argument. He points out that even if there is no shift of expenditure from one field to another, a rise in price reduces the quantity of goods that can be bought with the *same* expenditure of money, and a reduction in price enables more to be bought. It will therefore still be true that when people try to buy more than is available, the resulting rise in prices and wages automatically corrects this; and whenever people spend too little, a reduction in prices and wages would enable them to buy more goods with the same expenditure. An excessive or deficient demand would still be corrected by the automatic movement of prices and wages in a free market and the "genuine" wage, and prosperity without inflation, would still be reached automatically.

Unfortunately this second argument will not do either. If prices and wages are reduced in the economy as a whole, total income and spending *cannot* remain the same. At the lower prices and wages, less income is received by the producers of each unit of output. Since prices in general have fallen, income in general is cut and spending in general will be reduced in a similar proportion. With income reduced just as much as prices, there is no reason why more goods will be bought than before.

The same thing is true when spending is excessive. A general rise in prices increases the income of the producers and sellers in the same proportion. Since, in a general inflation, this is happening to everybody—i.e., to producers in general—income in general increases and spending in general increases so that the inflation in general can go on.

We may now look more closely at the reasons why these two allegedly automatic forces fail to correct an excess or deficiency of demand in the economy as a whole. The first, which we may call the *substitution effect,* is very potent for a limited part of the economy. An excess of demand for the product over the supply causes prices and wages to rise through the reactions of the buyers and sellers on the market. The price rise causes customers to *substitute* other products that have not become more expensive; the wage increase causes managers to substitute machinery and materials made by other workers whose wages have not risen and causes workers to move into this part of the economy from other areas where wages have not risen. But the substitution effect does not work for a *general* inflation because there is nothing to substitute. *Everything* has be-

HOW THE MONEY GOES ROUND

come more expensive. Conversely, when there is a deficiency of demand in a sector of the economy and prices and wages fall the same substitutions will work in the opposite direction. But if there is a *general* depression and *all* prices and wages fall, there is again no reason for any substitution, there is no substitution effect and the automatic cure for the depression by cutting wages does not work.

All this is a matter of *degree,* possibly somewhat obscured by our having considered so far only the two extreme cases. At the one end we have a change in prices and wages in a very small area of the economy so that *all* the possible substitutions would come into play; all the other products to or from which the consumers could shift, all the machinery and materials which can in some degree replace or be replaced by labor in the area, and all the other industries from which labor and other resources could be drawn, or for which labor and other resources would be released, by a difference in wages or prices or profits. At the other extreme, we have a change in prices and wages in the economy as a whole when *none* of these substitutions or shifts can take place. But there are also all the intermediate degrees. An inflation or deflation of wages and prices in a whole sector of the economy does not mobilize those substitutions or shifts that would have taken place *within* this sector if the prices and wages had changed only in a small part of it, but it does induce substitutions or shifts between the inflated or deflated sector and the rest of the economy. The larger the inflated or deflated sector, the smaller the remaining area, not only absolutely but even more so relatively to the former, and the less important will be the remaining possible substitutions or shifts. When the inflated or deflated area extends to cover the whole economy, the remaining substitution possibilities vanish completely and there is no substitution effect at all. The substitution effect argument is *inappropriate* to a *general* excess or deficiency of demand.

The second force that allegedly works automatically to correct an excess or a deficiency of demand we may call the *real income* effect. A price increase reduces the real income of anyone whose money income is unchanged—he cannot buy as much as before; and a fall in prices raises his real income—it enables him to buy more than before.

For a small section of the economy the real income effect is too tiny to count. Consider an item on which the whole economy spends as much as $\frac{1}{100}$ of its income. This would be an enormous industry with sales of $4 *billion* in the United States. A 10 per cent price cut in this industry would raise real income in the economy by 10 per cent of that $\frac{1}{100}$, i.e., by $\frac{1}{1000}$. If the proportion of real income spent on the cheapened product is unchanged (in the absence of any substitution effect it could just as well be decreased as increased) the demand for the products of this sector would increase by $\frac{1}{100}$ of the $\frac{1}{1000}$ increase in national real income. This amounts to $\frac{1}{100,000}$ of the national income or about $4 *million*—$\frac{1}{1000}$ or $\frac{1}{10}$ of one per cent of the sales of the industry.

For a smaller industry or firm the effect would be much more than proportionately smaller. (It would vary as the *square* of sales.) For an industry or firm with $4 *million* of sales in the United States, or $\frac{1}{100,000}$ of the national income, a 10 per cent price cut would increase the national real income by 10 per cent of that $\frac{1}{100,000}$, i.e., by $\frac{1}{1,000,000}$. If the economy then, in the absence of any substitution effects, spent the same proportion as before of its greater real income on this firm or industry, the increase in sales would amount to $\frac{1}{100,000}$ of the $\frac{1}{1,000,000}$ increase in the national real income. This amounts to $\frac{1}{100,000,000,000}$ of the national real income or about $4.00 (four dollars and no cents)! The same figure would measure the decrease in demand for the product of an industry on account of the real income effect from a 10 per cent price increase.

HOW THE MONEY GOES ROUND

The real income effect is clearly not of a magnitude that would seem significant to any businessman. But if all prices are changed at the same time (in response, say, to a general inflation or depression), the real income effect is no longer insignificant. If money income remains the same, the argument goes, a ten per cent over-all price cut would increase real income by about ten per cent. (More accurately, by one ninth—i.e., if prices are cut in the proportion of 100:90, the real income rises in the proportion 90:100.) The rise in prices and wages resulting from an excess of demand would automatically reduce and then eliminate the excess demand, and a fall in prices and wages resulting from a deficiency of demand would automatically cure the deficiency of demand.

The real income effect would not work in this way, however, because money income would *not* remain the same. A general price increase would also constitute an increase in *money income* from the same real sales of goods and services—we may call this the *money income effect*—which would cancel out the effect of the price increase. There would be *no* reduction in the real income, no real income effect and no correction or mitigation of the excess demand. Similarly, a price cut would not alleviate the deficiency of demand. There would be a reduction in *money income* from the same real sales of goods and services and this *money income effect* would cancel any effects of the price cut on real income.

It is true that any businessman in considering the effects of a change in the price of his product or in the wage he pays would legitimately and reasonably neglect the money income effect. It would be of the same order of magnitude as the real income effect and equally negligible. From the over-all point of view, it is necessary to take into account both the real income effect and the money income effect of the change in price. Neither is negligible. But when this is done, it is seen that the two cancel out. What is not permissible is to adopt the over-all point of view in order to take into account the real income effect and then to shift to the individual point of view in order to disregard the cancelling money income effect. It is this illegitimate and illogical shift in the point of view that makes the "real income effect" look like an automatic cure for inflation and for depression.

The desire to believe that there, nevertheless, *must* be a satisfactory automatic mechanism for achieving prosperity without inflation cannot be exorcised by mere logic or even by logic combined with experience. The feeling that what is true for each firm or industry must be true for all of them together is too strong. The facts of depressions and inflations can be blamed on faulty policy preventing the automatic mechanism from working, and every time the theory or explanation of how the mechanism should do the job is shown to be in error, it is possible to look for another theory to take its place.

A more sophisticated theory is sometimes put forward to take the place of the two just counted out and to justify the idea that there is after all an automatic cure in the system for inflation and depression. This third theory is neither inappropriate (as is the first argument based on the substitution effect) nor illogical (as is the second argument based on an illegitimate switching between the particular and the general points of view). The third theory is merely unpractical. It is based on a remarkable over-emphasis on the probable effects of changes in the real value or purchasing power of the stock of money in circulation.

If prices keep on rising in an inflation and incomes rise with prices, but the amount of money stays the same, this amount of money ultimately becomes insufficient to carry on the ordinary activities of business. A larger stock of money is then needed and the public tries to increase its stocks of money. The public as a whole cannot succeed in increasing the stock of money; in a modern economy only the monetary authorities can do that. The individuals and businesses that constitute the public can only get money from each other, and this does not affect the total stock. But in the course of individuals or businesses *trying* to increase their own holdings of money at the expense of each other, they may spend less money or they may borrow money to add to their money stocks, thus making it harder for others to borrow money to spend. When this has happened to a sufficient degree, spending is no longer excessive and the inflation has automatically come to an end.

In the same way, when there is a depression and prices fall, an unchanged money stock becomes excessive in real value or purchasing power. That is to say, people don't need so much cash at the lower price and income levels, and they try to get rid of some of the surplus cash. The public as a whole cannot succeed in doing that since the total supply of money is determined not by them but by the monetary authorities. But in the course of trying to unload the cash on each other they may spend more money or they may lend more readily, thus making it easier for others to borrow to spend more. When this has gone far enough the depression has automatically been cured.

On this theory, which we may call the *real cash balances* theory, the automatic cure does not depend on a change in wages relatively to prices—as it does in the first theory—or on a change in prices relatively to incomes—as it does in the second theory. The third theory recognizes that wages and prices and incomes would move together. Its automatic cure depends (a) on wages, prices and incomes all moving together relatively to the stock of money (which is unchanged in nominal terms, i.e., in Dollars, Pounds or Pesos), (b) on this movement increasing or decreasing the need for money or cash balances relatively to the available stock, and (c) on the effects on the level of spending in the economy of the (necessarily futile) attempts on the part of individuals and businesses to increase their cash balances by getting the cash from each other and to decrease their cash balances by unloading cash on each other.

But these forces are not nearly powerful enough to warrant reliance on them as a satisfactory practical mechanism for the automatic cure of inflation or depression. When we look at what has happened in inflations in other countries, we see that it is possible, with the existing stock of money, for prices to rise to many times their present level, i.e., by hundreds of percentage points, before the amount of money becomes impossibly insufficient. Long before inflation has gone that far something else would have happened to upset the apple cart.

The same thing is true in reverse. To cure a depression, prices would have to fall until the buying power of the existing stock of money had increased to the extent required to increase purchases by as much as is needed to give work to all the unemployed. For example, if the real value or purchasing power of the stock of money needs to be increased threefold in order to have the desired effect on purchases, prices would have to fall by two-thirds—i.e., they would have to fall to one-third of what they were in the beginning.

But prices do not fall easily. It takes severe and continued depression to force them down. Even the great depression of the 1930's reduced prices hardly at all in Great Britain. In the United States prices did fall by about one-third, but even this did nothing significant toward solving the depression. When we consider that the forces resisting price reductions—the trade unions and business organizations—are much stronger now than they were then, it becomes clear that long before any depression has succeeded in reducing prices by two-thirds everything would have been swept away by ruin and revolution.

This would perhaps not be so if a moderate degree of depression would make prices and wages fall rapidly to the required level. But no matter what practices are adopted there will remain powerful resistances to wage cuts in any democratic country. The persistence of the depression would finally force some wages to give way, but each group would try hard to be the last so that they could gain from lower prices before they contributed their own wage and income cut. This would establish an expectation of further reductions in prices and wages and a climate in which it would be wise (for each individual) to postpone as much expenditure as possible. Such postponement of spending would intensify the depression. It would have to get much worse before it could get better. And the same thing would be true in reverse for an excess in demand.

When this is realized, there is a temptation to resort to appeals to the public to increase (or to decrease) spending. This doesn't work at all. If there is too much spending, it will not help if we are told, no matter how dramatically, over the radio or television or in the newspaper that the inflation that threatens would be stopped if everybody were to spend less. We would probably do just the opposite. We would say it really is too bad that everybody is spending too much and that we're going to have inflation; everybody really ought to spend less. But each of us would meanwhile make a point of buying that suit of clothes or that dress before it became even more expensive. Everyone else would do the same; so that instead of spending less, everyone would spend more.

HOW THE MONEY GOES ROUND

Exactly the same thing would happen in reverse in a depression. If everyone is asked to spend more because depression threatened, most people would wait—either in order to buy more cheaply later, or in order to build up a reserve against evil days. The result would be not more spending but still less spending, and the depression would get worse. Publicity and enlightenment are no cure for excess or deficiency of spending. It just happens that self-interest, and *especially* enlightened self-interest, is contrary to the general interest and works to aggravate and not to cure the disorders.

But there is no reason to despair. Activities which benefit the individual are frequently not in the general interest and quite often activities which are in the general interest are not privately profitable. There is a device which has been developed to deal with just that kind of situation. This device is *government*. When something important needs to be done but no individual gets around to doing it, we form a government to do it for the community.

If total spending is too little, and individuals (possibly for excellent personal reasons) do not respond to appeals to spend more, and it takes too long and too painful a depression to induce increased purchases by the "real cash balance" route via deflation, the government can come to the rescue with a "prosperity policy." The government can spend more itself; it can make it easier for people to borrow money and spend it (usually for investment); it can reduce taxes so that people have more money left to spend; and it can distribute more money in pensions or subsidies so as to increase spending by the beneficiaries. And it can do each of these things in reverse if it is desirable to reduce spending. When there is too much spending, the government can spend less itself; it can make it harder for people to borrow so they are induced to spend less; it can tax people more so they have to spend less; and it can reduce subsidies thereby reducing expenditure by the beneficiaries. In effect, the government can adjust the total rate of spending until it is neither too great nor too small and we have neither an excess nor a deficiency of demand.

This is not "a theory of deficit spending." A governmental prosperity policy for preventing depression and inflation is often mistakenly so called because our understanding of it was largely gained during the 1930's when there was a depression and the need was for the government to increase spending, which would result in a deficit. But the prosperity policy is just as applicable when spending is excessive, and then it would result in a surplus. It is not a system of deficits any more than it is a system of surpluses. It is a system of *balance*. To be sure it would lead to chronic deficits if spending were chronically insufficient and the government had to keep on spending more than it raised in taxes in order to prevent depressions. But it would lead to chronic surpluses if spending were chronically excessive and the government had to keep on taxing more than it was spending in order to prevent inflation.

The recognition of governmental responsibility for prosperity is not tied to a particular philosophy of government. Democrats and Republicans alike want to maintain prosperity, and no matter what the government of the United States in the future, it will recognize and act on this responsibility, some governments perhaps a little more readily than others, but all governments before depression or inflation becomes severe.

This is not so much because our rulers have been educated. It is rather because the public has experienced the prosperity policy in action, though unfortunately only in a rather special connection. Everybody has seen how prosperity is brought about during war and in preparation for war by government expenditure on armaments. Nobody has been able to give a sensible reason why the same prosperity would not prevail, under much happier circumstances, if the same expenditure were made on housing or roads or schools or hospitals. Workers would earn the same wages and business would make the same profits. The only difference is that instead of instruments of war and destruction we would have houses, roads, schools, and hospitals.

It is this recognition by the public which will make it impossible for any government in the future to refrain from taking action to prevent severe depression, even if the expenditure needed for prosperity is not enforced by the need for armaments. Enough people realize that prosperity can be maintained, and depression and inflation avoided, by governmental management of total spending; most people want prosperity to be maintained and depression and inflation to be avoided; and we live in a democratic society where the government serves the people and likes to be re-elected.

CHAPTER XI

SELLERS' INFLATION AND INFLATIONARY DEPRESSION*

In Chapter X, which deals with inflation and depression, these are treated in the more or less traditional way which assumes that inflation is caused by excess demand—by buyers trying to buy more goods and services than the economy can supply even when everybody can find all the work he wants. In the last few years a new kind of inflation has been attracting attention that seems to be able to flourish without excess demand.

In 1957, the United Automobile Workers International Union (UAW) invited the three big automobile corporations to lower the 1958 automobile prices as a first step in checking the inflationary process from which our economy was suffering. Not unnaturally, the corporations in effect replied, "After you, my dear Alphonse." Yet the proposals and counterproposals were something more than sparrings for better future bargaining positions. They clearly demonstrated three phenomena of the first importance: (1) a genuine concern, on both sides, with the dangers of inflation, (2) a readiness to cooperate in checking the inflation (provided that such cooperation was not exploited and diverted for the benefit of the other side), and (3) perhaps the most important, a recognition that the inflation was caused not by *buyers* trying to buy more of everything than could be supplied—by "too much money chasing too few goods"—but by *sellers* pressing for higher prices.

President Eisenhower recognized this when he made his appeal to labor and to business to help the fight against inflation by exercising restraint and refraining from demanding higher wages or prices. If inflation in general could be caused only by excess demand for goods by *buyers,* restraint by *sellers* (of products or of labor)

---

* This chapter is based on a paper delivered to the Johns Hopkins Political Economy Seminar on November 6, 1957, and condensed in an article in *Commentary,* February 1958, entitled "Halting the Current Recession."

would always be irrelevant and the President's appeal would be pointless. In the presence of excess demand by buyers, restraint by sellers would be ineffective, and in the absence of excess demand by buyers it would be unnecessary.

But excess demand by buyers is *not* the only possible cause of inflation. This is shown by the experience of rising prices while output was failing to keep up with our growing productive capacity, when we were perfectly capable of supplying much more than the current overall demand for goods and services, and when efforts by sellers to persuade the public to buy were as strenuous as ever. In such conditions price increases cannot be due to the pressure of *buyers* who are finding it difficult to buy. Prices are rising because of pressures by *sellers* who insist on increasing prices (even though they are finding it not so easy to sell). The inflation is not *buyer-induced* but *seller-induced*. We have not a *buyers' inflation* but *sellers' inflation*.

The authorities, in endeavoring to stop the inflation by applying budgetary retraint and tight money, have been very effective in removing excess demand, but have not completely removed the upward pressure on prices from the sellers' side. They have, however, been so effective in reducing demand that they have overdone this and removed some demand that was *not* in excess. They have brought about a condition of *deficient demand*—not enough demand to enable us to make full use of our productive potential. Nevertheless prices keep on rising. The net result is that we are now suffering at the same time from both inflation *and* depression —prices are rising and at the same time we are not fully utilizing our available labor force and productive potential.

This appears paradoxical only because of our habit of assuming that inflation, or rising prices, is always caused by excess demand, and many people still argue as if the only kind of inflation possible is demand inflation or buyers' inflation. Although they cannot deny that they see excesses of potential supply much more often than they see excesses of buyers' demand, they insist that "there ain't no such animal" as sellers' inflation. They declare that "inflation is inflation" and they sternly dismiss all talk about a new kind of inflation that does not respond to the orthodox treatment of monetary and fiscal restrictions as diversionary tricks by naughty children who are trying to dodge their medicine.

SELLERS' INFLATION

Unfortunately, such sternness is only too understandable. Some of the economists who were early to recognize the nature of sellers' inflation were so impressed by the impossibility of dealing with it by the orthodox instruments of monetary and fiscal policy that they capitulated to the temptation of dallying with "mild" or "moderate" inflation as part of an acceptable policy. The orthodox economists quite rightly point out that such a capitulation is indefensible either on moral or on practical grounds. Even a "mild" inflation accumulates, at "compound interest" and robs pensioners, fixed income receivers, and many other unfortunate victims, while it sabotages the proper calculations and accountings necessary for wise economic decisions. In time many of these faults could be corrected by institutional adjustments, but to keep the inflation "mild" is more difficult than to prevent the inflation from starting in the first place. The very same excuses for accepting "creeping" inflation instead of maintaining price stability would be even more seductive for permitting a "creeping" inflation to become a "walking" one. Stronger still would be the pressures for changing from a "walking" to a "running" inflation and for permitting a "running" inflation to break into a "gallop." Retreat only induces further retreat.

But the objections to appeasement do not in the least diminish the importance of recognizing the existence of sellers' inflation, for it is not the *recognition* of the existence of sellers' inflation but rather its *denial* that is dangerous. It is the belief that the medicines appropriate for buyers' inflation are the only medicines available, when joined with the discovery that these do not work, which give rise to defeatism and appeasement.

Another reason for reluctance to recognize sellers' inflation is that it has often been called "cost inflation" or "cost-push inflation" or "wage-cost inflation," giving the impression that the whole of the blame for it falls on labor or on trade unions. When trade unions raise wages by more than can be absorbed by increasing productivity, costs rise. The employer then seems to be completely innocent of "profit inflation" in passing on the increase in costs as long as he does not raise his markup, i.e., as long as he does not increase the prices he charges for the product in a greater proportion than his costs have increased. But a sellers' inflation could just as well be started by an increase not in the wages but in the markup. Prices would rise and wages would then be raised by workers in attempts to maintain (or restore) their original buying power. Business would then "innocently" raise their prices again only in proportion to the increase in their costs, and we would have the inflation upon us as well as endless dispute about who started it first—the famous chicken and egg.

The "who started it first" debate is a complete waste of time because there *is* no original situation in which there was a "just" or "normal" distribution of the product between wages and profits. Any change can be seen either as a disturbance of equilibrium or as the correction of an inequity—all depending on the point of view. The term "sellers' inflation," by treating wages and profits on exactly the same footing, avoids the mutual recrimination. Sellers' inflation takes place whenever wage-earners and profit-takers together attempt to get shares that amount to more than 100% of the selling price. It is futile to ask whether this is because the wages demanded are too high or whether it is because the profits insisted on are too great.

It is of course impossible for the sellers to get more than 100% of the proceeds but it is precisely on such an impossibility that any continuing process depends. Buyers' inflation is similarly built on trying for the impossible. In that case it is buyers trying *to buy more than 100%* of the goods available. Their attempt bids up prices. They do not (and cannot) succeed in buying more than 100% of the available goods, but they keep on trying and so we have the continuing process of buyers' inflation. In sellers' inflation it is the sellers who keep trying to get more than 100%, so they keep on raising wages and prices and we have the continuing process of sellers' inflation.

The resistance to recognizing sellers' inflation takes many forms. One argument is that there must have been some excess buyers' demand or prices could not have risen. This begs the whole question since it assumes what it wants to prove, namely, that the only possible cause of rising prices is excess buyers' demand.

A more sophisticated argument points out that as long as output shrinks less than prices increase (and this is usually the case), there must have been an increase in the total amount spent by the buyers. This is indisputable, but an *increase in expenditure* is not

SELLERS' INFLATION

the same thing as *excess demand*. An excess of demand by buyers is the *cause* of the price increase. An increase in expenditure could be the *result* of attempts by the authorities to keep down the unemployment induced by price increases imposed by sellers.

A still more sophisticated argument along the same lines is that if the authorities would only be resolute and not permit an increase in expenditure, the depression and unemployment resulting from a wage or price increase would stop the sellers from increasing prices. The question then is how much unemployment would be required and whether it is morally desirable or politically possible for the authorities to induce or permit unemployment of the required volume and duration.

Before considering this question it would be desirable to review briefly the main approaches to the general problem of inflation and depression.

First, there is the classical approach. This assumes perfectly flexible prices and wages, so that any excess of demand makes prices and wages rise, and any deficiency of demand makes prices and wages fall, until price stability and full employment are restored. Monetary and fiscal policy are unimportant. As long as the quantity of money is kept fairly stable by some automatic device such as the gold standard, the price level will automatically adjust itself so as to yield full employment with price stability and without inflation. The corresponding policy is *laissez faire*—do nothing.

The second is the Keynesian approach, developed by Keynes in the early 1930's, to take account of the fact that we do not have the degree of *downward* price and wage flexibility that is needed to make *laissez faire* a satisfactory policy. We have seen in Chapter X that the automatic cure depends not on wages falling relatively to prices or on wages and prices falling relatively to incomes but on wages, prices and incomes all falling relatively to the quantity of money. This process may take years of severe depression, so that the appropriate policy is to abandon *laissez faire*—not to wait for the price level to adjust itself to the quantity of money but to adjust the quantity of money to the price level.

This switch from *laissez faire* to an active monetary and fiscal policy also applies in the opposite direction to prevent *excess* demand or buyers' inflation. Instead of waiting for the price increase to *absorb* the excess demand it calls for monetary or fiscal policy to *remove* it, adjusting demand downward to the price level instead of waiting for the price level to rise until it has adjusted itself to the high level of demand.

The third approach takes account of the fact that an insufficiency of demand, even when causing considerable unemployment, may not only fail to make prices and wages fall quickly enough to provide the automatic (classical) cure, but may even be unable to prevent them from continuing to rise. When we have strong trade unions with the power to raise wages, strong corporations with the power to set prices administratively, and a general atmosphere in which it is considered normal, natural and only fair for wages to be increased regularly by more than the increase in productivity in the economy (plus or minus any increase or decrease in labor's share of the product), prices must increase and we have sellers' inflation. The widespread and generous feeling that workers are entitled to the increases in wages that they get is made much easier by a recognition that any raise need not be taken out of profits, since it is possible, as well as proper, to "pass it along" to the ultimate purchaser in higher prices. Indeed it is usually considered only right that profits, in dollars, should be *increased* so as to protect *real* profits from the declining value of the dollar.

We have already mentioned the argument that a really firm refusal on the part of the monetary authorities to permit the volume of expenditure to increase, no matter what happened, would bring the sellers to their senses. Realizing, or discovering, that they will not be able to sell so much if they raise their prices, they will refrain from raising prices and they will not grant, or ask for, wage increases that raise costs by more than can be squeezed out of profits. But the question is will they? Or rather how severe a state of depression and unemployment would have to be maintained in order to induce sellers not to use their power to raise prices, and how able and willing would the authorities be to bring about and maintain this degree of depression and unemployment?

An interesting indication of the strength of the most important element in the setup—the general feeling of the propriety and inevitability of continuing wage and cost increases (to be "passed on" in increased prices) was provided in the very debate about automobile prices and wages referred to earlier. The U.A.W. had asked the automobile corporations to reduce automobile prices by $100 in 1958, promising to take this into consideration when presenting their 1958 demands for wage increases. The counter-suggestion, clearly put forward as an extreme bargaining position, was deeply concerned with the danger of inflation. This counter-suggestion included the continuation of the previous contract which offered a regular wage increase of 2½% per annum in addition to a cost of living adjustment. But 2½% per annum is more than the average increase in output per head in the American economy, so that there was a significant piece of sellers' inflation right at the lower end of the range subject to negotiation. Another indication is provided by the outcome of the protracted steel strike of 1959 which the steel company fought under the flag of preventing inflation. The settlement was such that the main question remaining was whether or not the companies would be able to postpone the price increase until after the November 1960 elections.

In such an atmosphere it would require, one would think, a quite severe depression to change people's notions of what is the proper development of wage rates and of the corresponding prices (since the right of wages to increase goes together with the right of profits at least not to fall).

At the same time the avoidance of severe depressions seems to have won a firm place in the country's economic policy. With such a setup there is no need to worry whether the cure is worse than the disease —whether the depression would be more harmful than the inflation that it would prevent. This cure is not one that any government would seriously attempt to carry out.

All this brings us to the perhaps only too obvious conclusion that sellers' inflation cannot be cured or prevented by measures directed against excess demand by *buyers*. It can be successfully treated only by attacking the pressure on prices by sellers.[1]

In a perfectly competitive market the institutions and mores that

[1] In an outstanding article which concentrated on showing the inadequacy and superficiality of proposals to prevent inflation by monetary and fiscal policies and declarations, Professor Sumner H. Slichter seemed to suggest that the distinction between buyers' inflation and sellers' inflation is a futile fantasy. Thus he said (using somewhat different terminology) "Much time has been wasted in recent years in discussing whether inflation is demand-inspired or

give sellers the power to push prices up cannot exist. Prices cannot rise unless there is excess demand. If there is a deficient demand prices must fall. We cannot have inflation and depression at the same time.

But where prices are administered by decrees of large firms, and wages are administered by joint decrees of powerful unions together with powerful employers or employer groups, the situation is different. Sellers' inflation is a by-product of the process, and together with sellers' inflation we can also have depression—indeed we *will* have depression with our sellers' inflation if the authorities try to cure the inflation by reducing ("excess") demand.

These by-products of administered wages and prices have important similarities to, and are no less socially harmful than, the monopolistic exploitation that would result from unregulated administration of prices by private owners of public utilities. We have gone a long way towards eliminating the latter evil by *regulating* the prices set by public utilities. A similar device can be used to eliminate sellers' inflation. Just as public utility prices can be and are being regulated so as to prevent monopolistic exploitation, so administered prices and wages can and should be regulated so as to prevent sellers' inflation and the depression it may bring with it.

The regulation of administered prices and wages to prevent sellers' inflation would have to follow somewhat different lines. It would not be concerned with the rate of return on investments, nor would it regulate anything other than *price*. The purpose of the regulation would be only to prevent *restrictive prices* or *restrictive wages* from

---

cost-inspired. (Some 70 or 80 years ago the Austrian theory of value produced a similar debate as to whether demand or cost determines value; the argument ended suddenly when it dawned on the economists that each blade in a pair of scissors cuts.)" ("On the Side of Inflation," *Harvard Business Review*, Sept./Oct. 1957, p. 32.)

However, the inapplicability of this analogy jumps to the eye in his very next sentence which shows that it *can* make sense to distinguish between the "blades," since he went on to say, "Thus changes in the price level may originate either with shifts in the demand schedules or with shifts in the supply schedules." And in another article, Professor Slichter definitely aligned himself with the "sellers' inflation" blade in declaring that, "There is no evidence that prices are rising ahead of costs and are pulling costs up. The evidence is all the other way: that prices are being sluggishly adjusted to slowly rising costs." ("Government Spending Can Reduce Taxes," *Harvard Business Review*, July/Aug. 1957, p. 106.)

SELLERS' INFLATION

being administered. A restrictive price is one that results in the demand for a product falling below capacity output. A restrictive wage is one that results in less than full employment in the specific labor market to which it applies. With monetary and fiscal policy concentrating on maintaining adequate buyers' demand for full employment while preventing buyers' inflation, it would be possible to maintain a stable price level while wages rose on the average at the same rate as productivity.

To achieve this, the regulatory body, following a set of rules, would have to do the following things:

(1) Permit an administered price increase only when production and sales are at capacity. Such price increases should not be withheld on account of profits being high.

(2) Enforce decreases in administered prices whenever production and sales are significantly below capacity. A price decrease should not be waived on account of profits being low (or even negative) as long as the price more than covers current operating costs (more exactly, short period marginal costs).

(3) Permit increases in wages in general at a rate equal to the average trend of increase in national productivity.

(4) Permit increases in administered wages greater than this only where the labor market is significantly tighter than on the average—e.g., where unemployment is less than half the national average.

(5) Permit only smaller increases in administered wages, or no increases at all, wherever the labor market is significantly slacker than on the average—e.g., where unemployment is more than twice the national average. (Some prices must fall if others rise if there is to be price level stability but it is possible to avoid reductions in money wages because of increasing productivity.)

This is of course not a fully worked out solution ready for immediate application. Much remains to be developed—such as generally acceptable criteria of capacity of different firms and industries and generally acceptable measures of slackness or tightness in particular labor markets. The regulations could be enforced by treating as nondeductible for income tax any unauthorized part of wages or of other costs paid out. The regulations would enforce more intense price competition. While making prices more "correct" they would also eliminate high cost firms (now sheltered by their more efficient competitors keeping prices above the "correct" level). While the public would benefit from the increased efficiency of the economy, such elimination of "competition by the inefficient" would conflict with special interests and with certain so-called anti-trust polices that are in effect anti-competition policies and need to be reconsidered.

There remain important problems of organization and administration of the regulatory body as well as the need for widespread and intensive public discussion to bring about the familiarity with, and the understanding of, the nature and purpose of the proposed regulation that is essential for its effective operation in a democracy. And in the course of such examination and debate important developments, changes and improvements are to be expected. Nevertheless the general lines indicated seem inevitable if sellers' inflation is to be attacked at its roots.

It is to be expected that one of the most powerful debating points against the proposed price (and wage) regulation will be the charge that it means *price control*. But price regulation is not price control —it is almost the exact opposite. Price control consists of an attempt by authority to *interfere* with the price mechanism by establishing a price below that which clears the market, i.e., below the "genuine" price, discussed in Chapters III, IV and V. Price regulation on the other hand rather *restores* the price mechanisms. It interferes only with interferences, preventing the monopolist or cartel or trade union or whoever else determines an administered price or wage, from setting it above the "correct" level.

The regulation of public utilities prices, by moving the actual price closer to the "correct" price without making them any less "genuine," increases output and leads to a more efficient use of the resources of the economy. The owners of the public utility are indeed deprived of monopoly profits, but the gain to consumers is much greater than the loss to the monopolists.

The regulation of administered prices and wages to prevent sellers' inflation would similarly establish prices that are both "genuine" and "correct" and compatible with full employment and price level stability. The cry of "price control" would be entirely without justification.

SELLERS' INFLATION

The restriction of output in the whole economy that results from attempts to curb sellers' inflation by reducing total spending, is more damaging than restriction of output by monopolistic public utilities. The latter shifts resources from producing more useful products to producing less useful products, while the former shifts resources from the production of useful products to producing nothing at all—except the human frustrations and suffering from unemployment. The regulation of prices and wages to prevent sellers' inflation is therefore more important than the regulation of monopolistic public utilities, and no more repugnant to the basic principles of the free, competitive society.

The full utilization of existing capacity may sometimes lead to inadequate profits, or even to losses, but that is the nature of the competitive *profit and loss* system. It shows that an error was made in the past in producing too much capacity in the industry, but that is no reason why society should not benefit from the use of the capacity once it has been produced. The low profits or the losses are then performing their proper function of discouraging further investment in such industries. In other cases the "genuine" prices—those that clear the market at full capacity output—will yield very large profits. The prices are nevertheless "correct" and the large profits are performing their proper function of encouraging more investment in such industries.

Just as low profits are no excuse for monopolistic restriction of output, so high profits are no excuse for enforcing price reductions below the "genuine" level. That *would* be price control and is to be equally condemned whether it is imposed by government or whether it is due to "restraint" on the part of producers who are powerful enough, and rich enough, to be able to do this. The existence of excess capacity in steel and in automobiles means that current prices are too high (to be "correct"). The emergence of gray and black market prices during and after World War II meant that prices were then too low (to be "genuine"). The generosity of the corporations at that time in selling too cheap (in part to privileged suppliers of the black market) is no justification for their selling too dear now. A defender of the free market or profit and loss system should not be appalled at the emergence either of profits or of losses.

It is possible that the trade unions would easily see all the social benefits from keeping the prices of products down to the level needed for capacity production and full employment, but would denounce the regulation of wages as an intolerable interference with the fundamental right of collective bargaining. It is possible that employers would quickly appreciate the desirability of curbing excessive wage demands but would reject the regulation of prices as an alien and unthinkable interference with the free economy and an impious infringement of the sacred rights of management in setting prices.

Such responses would indicate that "after you, my dear Alphonse" really means "include me out" or "let George do it," and that we would not have the cooperation that is necessary for success. But the true interests of labor would not be damaged by the trade unions' relinquishing the right to institute a sellers' inflation, nor would true interests of capital be betrayed by the loss of the same right. The justification of the free economy and its institutions rests ultimately not on any ancient divine rights but on their efficiency in satisfying the needs and the desires of a free people.

It has been very fashionable for some time to *deplore* inflation and to quote Lenin's declaration that inflation is the Achilles' heel or the Trojan Horse of capitalism. Recently it has become even more fashionable to *preach* restraint as a remedy for inflation to parties who cannot be expected to respond because they have no assurance that the others will play their part. The preaching seems to have stimulated many public declarations of conversion by Labor and Management to a readiness to *promise* restraint, provided the other parties cooperate. It is unlikely that the *deploring*, the *preaching*, the *declarations of conversion* or the *promises* will lead to any genuine results. The regulation of administered prices and wages would *provide* the restraint needed to protect the free economy from sellers' inflation and inflationary depression.

CHAPTER XII

RICH MAN, POOR MAN—
HOW MUCH INEQUALITY DO WE NEED?

In previous chapters, when discussing the prices of goods and services and the wages of labor, I have repeatedly asked the reader to disregard what the payments mean as income to people.

Here I want to keep the promise to consider the income aspect of the payments. In doing this I am afraid I shall annoy many people, both on the right and on the left. Conservatives will think that I am much too easy going about taking property and income away from people. On the other hand, many liberals or progressives will feel that I am trying too hard to justify the inequalities of capitalist society.

The sub-title of this chapter is, "How much inequality do we need?" How can we measure inequality? It is not at all easy. We cannot talk about a yard or a pint of inequality. Most of the difficulties don't appear if we talk about only two people. If one man has an income of ten thousand dollars a year and the other has twenty thousand, there is a certain degree of inequality. If they had incomes of five thousand and twenty-five thousand, we would say the inequality is greater. It is fairly easy to see here what is meant by a greater inequality. It is simply a greater ratio of the larger to the smaller number. But as soon as we get to three people, the problem becomes troublesome. Compare a situation where the three people have incomes of ten, fifteen, and twenty thousand dollars respectively, with another situation where they have ten, eleven, and twenty thousand. Has the inequality become greater, or less? Or is it the same? Take the case where the incomes are ten, nineteen, and twenty thousand dollars. Which of these arrangements are more equal and which are less equal?

Too often people pay attention to the incomes not of individual persons or families, but of organizations like corporations. I am not at all concerned about corporations being too rich or too poor.

A corporation is simply a large number of people doing something together somehow, and until we know what other incomes or wealth these people have, and how the income or the wealth of the corporation is divided among them, we haven't even begun to deal with the problem with which we are concerned, namely, the income or wealth of *people*. So I shall not talk at all in this connection about corporations or other organizations, considering them as being merely a part of the apparatus which influences the income or wealth or consumption of people through their receipt of dividends, interest, or salaries, and their ownership of stocks and bonds. I shall consider only the inequalities in the income or wealth of individuals or families.

What is the item whose inequality we want to measure? Are we more interested in inequality of wealth, which means all kinds of property, or are we interested in the amount of cash people have, on which we can get more reliable figures? Are we interested in their income—what they earn, their wages, salaries, dividends, rents received over a given period? Or are we concerned with how much people actually use up for their own consumption? We may begin with the distribution of *income* since the other measures, wealth, cash, and consumption, are all related to income in various ways.

Most people underestimate the inequality of income in one sense and overestimate it in another. They underestimate the range of inequality because it is very difficult to grasp how great is the distance between the poorest and the richest persons. On the other hand, the importance of the inequality in terms of the number of people involved and the degree to which their lives are affected by it is usually very much overestimated.

To picture the range of incomes among individuals, let a building block, one foot high, represent an income of one thousand dollars a year. A person having an income of two thousand dollars a year would be represented as standing on top of two blocks, one above the other, and a person with ten thousand dollars a year would be standing on a pile of ten blocks, and so on. If we put the tallest piles in the middle our blocks would form a kind of pyramid representing the distribution of income in, say, the United States.

This pyramid would not look a bit like the Egyptian pyramids. A majority of the people would be standing less than three feet above ground, and more than nine tenths of all the people in the United

States would be standing on piles less than six feet high, so that a tall man standing on the ground would be able to peep at their shoes. But the top of the pyramid would be lost in the clouds. The man with an income of a million dollars a year would be standing on a pile as tall as the Empire State Building, and the very richest man, with an income of thirty million dollars a year, would be six miles up in the sky, higher than the top of the tallest mountain in the world. The fact that people are impressed by such a demonstration only shows that they don't begin to realize how great is the range of incomes, or, in other words, what is meant by a million or ten million dollars.

But even so, most people in thinking of millionaires *overestimate* the *importance* of the inequality of incomes, astounding though it may be. There are relatively very few blocks higher than the third floor of an ordinary house because there are so few very rich people. The millionaires actually get only a very tiny part of the total income of the country. To get an idea of the true significance of the inequality, we may use another simple device called the Lorenz curve. This curve is easy to draw. Draw a square, then draw a straight line from the bottom left hand corner to the top right hand corner like this:

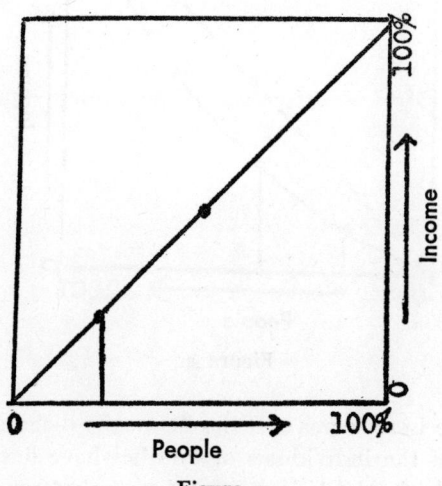

Figure 1.

This diagonal line will represent a perfectly equal distribution of income. Moving from the bottom left hand corner toward the right, the horizontal distance represents the population. If we go a quarter of the way from the bottom left hand corner toward the right, we have covered 25% of the population. The vertical distance, or the height of the point on the diagonal line above this 25% point, represents the percentage of the total income which goes to 25% of the population. We can easily see that on such a diagonal 25% of the people get 25% of the income, 50% of the people get 50% of the income, and so on all the way through, which is, of course, exactly what would happen if every individual or every family had exactly the same income.

If there is some inequality in incomes, we arrange the individuals or families in order, putting the poorer ones to the left. Then we get a line which hangs below the diagonal rather like a piece of string attached to the same corners as the diagonal but hanging down below it like this:

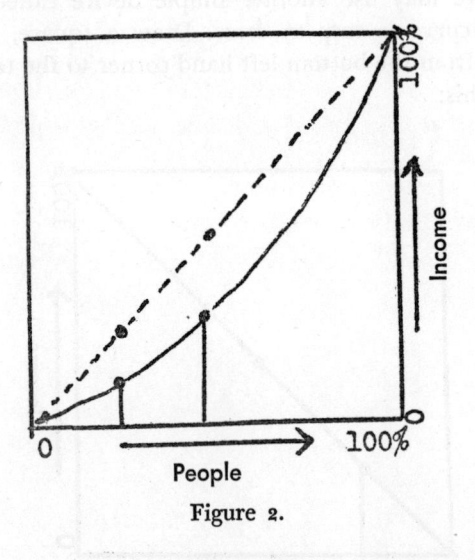

Figure 2.

This line is the Lorenz curve. It lies below the diagonal because the poorest 10% of the individuals or families have less than 10% of the total income, by definition, since they are poorer than the average. And the poorest 25% have less than 25% of the income, and so on. At every point the Lorenz curve will be below the diagonal for even the poorest 99% of the population who will have less than 99% of the total income. The poorest 99% will include many quite rich people since it includes everybody except the richest 1%, but their total income must be less than 99% of the total because the richest 1% of the people certainly have more than 1% of the total income—otherwise they would not be any richer than the others.

The degree of inequality is indicated by how far the Lorenz curve lies below the diagonal. The vertical distance between the diagonal and the Lorenz curves at any point represents the difference between the percentage of total income that the poorest X per cent of the population actually have and the X per cent of the total income that they would have if the income were divided with complete equality.

We can look at a few points on this Lorenz curve now, considering the distribution of income among *families*, rather than individuals, and choosing those that permit us to compare the poorest and the richest fifth of the families in the United States in 1954. The poorest fifth constitutes about nine million out of about 44 million families and includes all families earning less than $2300 a year. Instead of getting 20% of the total income, which they would get if it were divided equally, they get about 5% of it. The richest fifth, which includes all families earning above $7500 a year, gets about 43%. This has gone down from about 53% in the 1920's. The average income of the uppermost fifth is more than twice the national average, while the average income of the lowest fifth is about one-fourth the national average.

If we were to look at wealth, we would see a much greater inequality. But if we look at liquid cash held by families, we find that the poorest 20% of the families with 5% of the income have 9% of the cash, and that the richest 20% of families with 43% of the income have 57% of the cash. The poorest fifth do better in terms of the amount of cash they have than in terms of their income—and so does the upper fifth. There is a greater concentration of cash than of income at *both* ends.

This shows one way in which the significance of the inequality is exaggerated. The lowest fifth are not *all* such poor people. Some of them are well-to-do men who happen to have done badly in business this year. They have lots of cash and perhaps a lot of capital, but a negative income because they lost money instead of making a profit. And many other people of medium position who have been unlucky this year in one way or another are included here. This is borne out by the figures for consumption, which is of much more consequence than income. The poorest fifth consumes about 6% of total consumption even though their income is only about 5% of total income. Thus they are living on capital or on credit, and they couldn't do either of these if they were able to accumulate some savings to live on, or they are going to be richer next year so that they will be able to repay the credit.

At the other end, the upper fifth of the families, those who earn 43% of the total income, consume less than 30% of it. And for the very rich we would find a still greater discrepancy. People who earn millions of dollars don't usually consume millions of dollars; they wouldn't know how to. Instead they save it and invest it or give it away. They are, in fact, acting as agents for society. It is as if the wealth belonged to society at large, and they were merely looking after it on behalf of the rest of us.

We may not like that, of course. I would rather have the money myself. But I have to admit that if a millionaire has a great deal of income but doesn't consume much more than I do, I am probably not affected much differently than I would be if his wealth did not belong to him, but belonged to society at large or to a corporation of which I was a shareholder or to a cooperative society of which I was a member. The income saved and invested is used to build equipment, machinery, factories, enabling me and others to earn more money because we can then be more productive. It is a strange thing that many people who are disturbed because millionaires are so rich, are even more disturbed because those same millionaires don't consume all their income. They think it even more shameful that a millionaire saves a large part of his income because this makes him richer than ever. But if the rich never consumed more than ordinary people, saving and investing the rest of their income, their being rich would not harm anyone. It would only be a question of whether or not they were good investing agents.

In spite of what I have just said about the tendency to overestimate the importance of inequality, I find myself in agreement with the general opinion that there is too much inequality in this country. We have enacted progressive income taxes in recent decades, collecting more taxes—and not only more but in a larger proportion —from the rich.

We also have inheritance taxes which take away large percentages of large inheritances. These taxes, as well as taxes on corporations (which are mistakenly treated as if they were themselves rich people), are sometimes called redistributive taxes. This is a euphemism. The tax itself doesn't actually *redistribute* income. It only takes away income from rich people, and we have such taxes for the simple reason that we think nobody should be so rich.

There are some *indirect* redistributing effects of this taxation. To the degree that the rich are made to consume less, more is left for others to consume. But actually high taxes don't usually make rich people consume much less. In most cases they have enough left to maintain their usual standards of consumption. Because of the taxes they are not able to save and invest so much and the deficiency will have to be made up by somebody else—perhaps by the government —if our economic progress is to be maintained. There is therefore no redistribution from this in the sense of it permitting the poor to live better.

A much more effective and more useful way to reduce inequality is to eliminate the *causes* of inequality by removing the restrictions which prevent poor people from becoming richer, that is, from competing with those in privileged positions. The greatest equalizer is competition, competition of all kinds: competition for jobs as well as competition in business.

This leads me to mention one other aspect of inequality that is sometimes called exploitation. When the owner of a business makes a great deal of profit, it is often said that he is exploiting his workers. But in employing workers he is competing with others to employ them, and the *more* there are of such "exploiters," the higher the wages they all have to pay. At the same time, the more "exploiters" there are, the more goods they produce and try to sell, and the more they are forced to reduce prices because of competition. In a word, the greater the number of "exploiters" the less the "exploitation."

If competition has already reduced the margin between wages and prices so that any further narrowing would cause bankruptcy, raising wages could only have the effect of raising prices, and prices cannot be reduced without reducing wages. One can thus hardly speak of "exploitation" at all. Only where an unwarranted profit is made because competitors are being kept out, can we say there is exploitation, and the real cure for exploitation is to have more "exploiters."

Behind the concern for reducing inequality, whether through the taxation of the very rich or through the removal of hindrances to competition, there lies a moral judgment—a sentiment or feeling—that there is something good about equality. This feeling is very closely connected with the idea of democracy—of treating all people equally and fairly, and denying privileges to any groups or classes. In addition to the ideas of fairness and democracy, there is also a powerful argument for equality in terms of efficiency. If the purpose of income is to satisfy the needs of people, and if we want to satisfy those needs as effectively as possible, then it would seem wasteful or inefficient to satisfy relatively unimportant desires or preferences or whims of rich people and not the important needs of poor people. In the absence of special knowledge of special needs, it would seem that the most sensible thing would be to divide income equally so that it would tend to be used where it could contribute most towards satisfying the needs of most people. More extreme redistribution would, indeed, force the better-off to consume less and enable the poorer to consume more, and relatively unimportant needs will have been well sacrificed to permit the satisfaction of relatively important needs. But there are apparently very few people who want to establish complete equality of income.

In the extreme case, complete equality of income may even appear to be quite unfair. If one man chooses to do some extra work in the evenings or on weekends in his own garden and thus raises his income, we would not think it fair if he were not allowed to have more income than another man who doesn't undertake this extra work. Another way of expressing this is to say that the inequality is not real, but only apparent. The man who works more gives up his leisure because he would rather enjoy the vegetables he gets from his garden, or the appearance of a nicely painted house than the leisure he gives up for their sake. The man who works less gives up these vegetables and the beauty of his house. He prefers to have his leisure. Each could do what the other does if he wished to, so that in a more real sense there *is* equality. The goods and leisure they obtain are different only in the way that different goods may be bought by different people with the same money income. In the same category are inequalities of pay which come about because work is different in the degree of pleasantness or comfort or safety. As long as there is complete freedom for workers to move between the different occupations, such differences in pay do not constitute genuine inequality.

Then there are some *genuine* inequalities of pay that seem to most people to be justified. A person may earn more, even though his work is not *more* unpleasant or unsafe, yet the inequalities may be justified because a great deal of training is necessary for his work. The individual or his parents had to make sacrifices in connection with his training to acquire the special skills. This limits the number of people who can get into these occupations, and their scarcity makes their pay higher. One must, of course, distinguish between this and the case where, whether by direct or indirect means, the people in an occupation impose unnecessary restrictions and difficulties in the way of outsiders who would like to come in and compete with them.

There are several other kinds of inequality which also seem perfectly justifiable from the social point of view. A man may prefer not to consume all his income as soon as he gets it, but to postpone his consumption so as to consume more in the future instead. This postponement involves no sacrifice on anybody else's part and there is no injustice or unfairness or lack of democracy involved in it. Furthermore, the person who postpones his consumption may later increase it by more than he reduced it in the first place, so that his *total* consumption is greater. Yet even this does no harm to other people, which is our basic criterion, if his decision to save and invest instead of consuming, enables the total product of society to be improved or increased. This is what happens whenever a diminution of consumption permits an improvement in productive equipment to be made instead of the consumption goods. Later, when there is a larger output, a greater consumption can be enjoyed by the man who has made possible this greater output. Other people are no worse off than if he had not saved and invested but simply consumed his income in the first place.

Certain inequalities of income are therefore justifiable, necessary, and socially useful. They induce people to acquire useful skills, to undertake less pleasant but necessary work, and to postpone consumption whenever this would enable society to build up equipment to increase productivity. Wherever inequalities serve these functions, we may call them "functional inequalities."

We may formulate a sort of ideal by saying that we would like to have a society in which only "functional inequalities" exist; and also, we would have to say, a society in which these functional inequalities are of the right size. For they must not only not be too large, but they must also not be too small. In Great Britain, for example, a few years ago there was insufficient incentive for workers to work overtime or to move to more useful occupations. This led the Labour Government to reduce income tax on overtime pay. In the opinion of the Labour Government and, indeed, of almost everybody in Great Britain, the previously existing inequalities of pay were insufficient to perform their function. In the Soviet Union, which started in 1917 with the idea of abolishing all inequalities, there are now inequalities as great as those in the United States. These inequalities are of much more serious consequences in a human sense because, with the lower level of income generally, they make for much more grievous suffering by those at the bottom of the scale. Most people, therefore, believe that the degree of inequality in the Soviet Union is too great, just as it was apparently too small in Great Britain. In the United States the inequalities taken as a whole may be too great, but there are many cases in which the inequalities are insufficient.

One of the problems of the United States is that there are large areas, to a great extent in the South, where there is a great deal more labor compared to capital and resources than in other parts of the country. The cure for this is for labor to move to other areas where there is more capital compared to labor, and for capital to move into this area to equalize the proportions. Such movements would increase the efficiency of the country as a whole, raise the overall standard of living, and eventually result in a diminution of the inequality by removing its causes. It is a serious mistake, however, for wages to be equalized by *edict* between such areas, whether by the government or by nation-wide trade unions. This would remove a *functional* inequality since the inequality is performing the function of inducing labor to go north and inducing capital to go south. If this functional inequality were eliminated before it had completed the task, workers would stay in the South with promise of good pay and yet remain largely unemployed, for the capital would stay out. The efficiency of the economy as a whole would be less, and wages and profits in general would be lower, because there would be temporarily too little inequality.

We cannot get a numerical or quantitative answer to the question of how much inequality we need. But we can get a general indication of what to aim at. It would seem best to try to remove all inequalities which are not functional and which are due to restrictions, allowing functional inequalities to regulate themselves without legislative interference. There would then be a smaller need for the direct equalization of income and wealth by progressive taxation.

CHAPTER XIII

THE NATIONAL DEBT—
DO WE OWE IT TO OURSELVES?

When an editor of a newspaper or a cartoonist runs out of ideas, he can always call attention to the "national debt." The cartoonist can show the citizen being crushed by an enormous burden. The editorial writer will express himself arithmetically. Since nobody knows what is meant by a million dollars, let alone two hundred and ninety billions of dollars, the arithmetic can be very impressive. For example, he might ask how long you thought it would take you to pay off the national debt if you were given a full-time job of repaying it at the rate of one dollar every second. Years? Maybe hundreds of years? Not so easy. To pay out two hundred and ninety billion dollars at one dollar per second for seven hours a day working three hundred days a year would take about 40,000 years. And at the end of the 40,000 years would the national debt have disappeared? On the contrary, all this repayment would not even have begun to make a dent on the compounding of the debt into really astronomic trillions of trillions of dollars. It would take a *thousand* people each paying out a dollar a second just to pay off the interest so as to stop the debt from growing any bigger than the accumulated unpaid interest.

On Mondays, Wednesdays and Fridays the editorials frighten us with these unimaginably large numbers and tell us that the country is being destroyed by the tremendous national debt. But on Tuesdays, Thursdays and Saturdays the same editorial page will remind us that we are enjoying a higher standard of living and greater prosperity than ever before. If we remembered Monday's editorial on Tuesday we might wonder how we are able to manage so well in spite of the national debt and whether this could possibly be because we owe it only to ourselves.

Editorials dismiss the notion that we owe the national debt to ourselves as too ridiculous to deserve further analysis, and continue

THE NATIONAL DEBT

their arithmetical exercises. But when the scoffing and the arithmetic are over, the question still remains, "If we do not owe the national debt to ourselves, to whom *do* we owe it?" To this there is no answer. There *is nobody else* to whom we owe the debt. The national debt is a debt which the people in the United States owe, through the government, to the holders of the government bonds who, with some insignificant exceptions, happen to be the people in the U. S. No matter how funny it may seem to some, we don't owe it to Germany or Japan or Russia or any other country. We do, as a nation, owe the national debt to ourselves.

Our owing it to ourselves has important consequences. First, there is no analogy between the national debt and a private, personal, or business debt. If I have a personal debt, I am that much poorer. The man to whom I owe this debt can ask me to pay it at some time. If I pay him, it is a sacrifice on my part, and it may come at an extremely inconvenient time. The payment of my private debt means, for a time, consuming and enjoying less than I would otherwise be able to. I may have to tighten my belt.

But if part of the national debt is repaid, it is not true that the nation has to tighten its belt. The productive resources of the country are no less; the amount of goods produced is not diminished. What happens when a part of the national debt is repaid is that some money is taken from some of the inhabitants of the country and is given to others. The nation as a whole does not have to consume any less than before.

The analogy between personal debt and national debt is false because a personal debt is really an *inter-personal* debt—a debt of one person to another. The proper analogy to a personal debt is an *international* debt—a debt of one nation to another. The paying nation then does have to tighten its belt. But, it must be impressed upon the reader, a national debt is completely different, and repaying it does not involve any tightening of the national belt.

This would not sound so surprising if we remembered that there is the same difference when national and personal debts are *incurred*. When I incur a *personal* debt, the borrowed money enables me to consume more than I produce and earn myself. This is not true of *national* debt. Since the lenders are also inhabitants of the country, the borrowing of national debt only means a transfer among consumers and investors within the country (including the government as a consumer or investor on behalf of the public). The borrowing does not enable the nation to consume more than it produces. It does not allow the nation to loosen its belt in the first place and that is why it does not force it to tighten it again when the debt is repaid.

Yet it would be false to give the impression that the national debt doesn't matter at all. It is important to distinguish between the imaginary effects and the real effects of the national debt and to deny only the imaginary effects. But to many people the denial of imaginary effects looks like a denial of *all* the effects. This is sometimes the fault of those who deny the imaginary effects in using unnecessarily strong language. They tend to speak rather like a person whose twisted ankle has been exaggerated by rumor into a near fatality. He is tempted to say "Why it's nothing at all!" He doesn't really mean it is nothing at all; a twisted ankle can be extremely painful. He merely means to say that the other story is quite false. In the same way, to deny the imaginary effects of national debt is not to imply that there are no real effects to be concerned about.

The first imaginary effect I want to deal with is the notion that national debt is a national impoverishment. People speak as if the United States is poorer by two hundred and ninety billion dollars, the size of its national debt, just as any individual is poorer by the amount of his personal debt. To show his "net worth" in his balance sheet, the individual must subtract his debts from his assets. The mistake in applying this procedure to the nation is in forgetting that every debit has a credit.

If anybody owes money, there is somebody to whom the money is owed. This is always the case; there are no exceptions. The wealth of the nation includes the net worth of all the individuals in it, yet the nation is never poorer on account of a private debt by one individual in the country to another. This is because although the debt must be subtracted to get the figure for the net worth of the debtor, it must be added to get the figure for the net worth of the creditor, and the two items cancel when they are added in to show the wealth of the nation. And when the debt is paid, again the nation is not impoverished because the creditor receives all the money that the debtor pays, and the two opposite aspects of the transfer are equally part of the account of the nation.

All this seems to be very well understood by almost everybody, *but only for private* debt. Yet it applies in exactly the same way to public debt. For every dollar which you and I as residents of the United States owe, through our government, to the owners of the national debt, there is a corresponding creditor who owns a United States debt certificate of one kind or another. When we total the debt, it is our duty, if we do not want to mislead, to total the credit too. And if we count both, they cancel out.

While it is common for only the debit side of the national debt to be counted, I don't know of anybody who has counted only the credit side. But it could be said with equal logic, or rather illogic, that the United States is *richer* because among the things which Americans own are two hundred and ninety billions of national debt—in the form of first-class, gilt-edged securities guaranteed by the United States government. You can repeat the arithmetical exercises of the editorialist and see how long it would take to count this part of our *wealth*. This, of course, would be just as silly as doing the opposite. The United States is not any richer on account of the national debt than it is poorer because of it. Against the credit there is a debit, just as against the debit there is a credit.

It is commonly stated that the national debt will lead the United States to bankruptcy. What does this mean? A person is bankrupt if he cannot meet the demands of his creditors, is brought into court and declared bankrupt by a judge. He then knows that if he were to borrow any more money without warning the lender that he has been declared bankrupt, he could be sent to jail. It is prefectly clear that this couldn't be done by any judge to the United States. In the first place, the United States government can always legally meet its obligations by creating legal-tender money— and it is not illegal for the government to do that, even though it is illegal for anybody else. And in the second place, if for any reason the United States should refuse to meet any of its obligations, nobody has the power to do anything about it.

At this point the argument is generally changed and bankruptcy is declared to mean not bankruptcy, but a decline of the purchasing power of the dollar, which is quite a different and very serious thing. The national debt can contribute to a rise in prices, which means a fall in the value of the dollar. It may do this to a large or to a small degree, or not at all, depending upon many other factors, but we can only deal with this problem if we are clear that we are talking about changes in prices, and not about bankruptcy. I shall discuss such effects on prices later in dealing with the possible *real* effects of the national debt.

Another bogey is the question of what will happen when the national debt has to be repaid. One answer to this we have already given. If and when the repayment is made, the repayment will be received by people in this country and there will be no net deprivation involved for the country as a whole. The other and perhaps more important answer is that there is no date when the national debt has to be repaid. It is, of course, true that government bonds fall due at certain dates, but this does not mean that new bonds cannot then be issued—often even to the very same people. Many owners of national debt would be very unhappy if they could not re-invest the money all over again in the same way and for the same reasons as before.

There is a possibility of a sudden loss of confidence in the government and people may then want to cash in their government securities. It would be a very serious matter for any individual or corporation if it were suddenly called on to pay off its creditors in cash; but not for the government. This is because the government can create the money people want to hold instead of government bonds, and everybody can be happy. People who want cash can have cash, and as long as they only want to hold on to the cash no harm is done; the government may also feel happier because it now does not have to pay so much interest. On the other hand, people may not want to hold the money, but may decide to spend it. This could cause some real troubles which will soon be considered.

Another argument—and this one is quite a tear-jerker—is that the national debt will be a burden on our grandchildren, and that it is immoral and heartless of us to allow posterity to pay for our profligacy. This is nothing but an echo of the original confusion. If the debt should be repaid by our grandchildren, it is hard to see who would be receiving the repayment except our grandchildren. There is, besides, the other question as to whether or not the debt would in fact ever need to be paid off, and this applies just as much in our grandchildren's time as in the present.

At this point in the argument, there usually comes a bothersome snag phrased something like this: "Well, the mere existence of the national debt may not be so dangerous, nor is it likely to be called on to be repaid, and if it is we can probably handle that all right, but what about the *interest* on the national debt?" This is perhaps the most curious of all the objections. The man who brings it up is like a woodsman miraculously still sitting up in the air on a tree branch which he has sawed off. If the mere existence of the national debt doesn't do any harm, then there is no need for one to worry about the interest. One way of dealing with the interest is to borrow more money with which to pay it. All that would happen then is an increase in the national debt—which, it has been demonstrated, itself does no harm.

The apparent danger, or wickedness, or the profligacy of a person's spending more than his income—from which we get the false analogy to national debt—seems to apply doubly in the case of interest. I am not only failing to repay my debt, but I am actually getting deeper into debt meeting the interest. This is so doubly dangerous a course of behavior for any individual that it is twice as hard to remember that it is different for the nation. But the logic applied previously cannot be avoided here. The interest payments, just like national debt repayments, are paid by Americans to Americans. The nation as a whole is not impoverished by the interest payments any more than it is enriched by them.

Another objection we have to meet is that of the person who points to the physical destruction during the wars when most of our debt was incurred, and our failure to build houses or factories during these times. This lack is pointed to as constituting the real burden of the national debt on our children and grandchildren. The answer to this is that the destruction and failure to reconstruct will undoubtedly be a very real burden on our children and grandchildren. Many people in Europe and other parts of the world have suffered cruelly because of it. But the destruction would have been just as bad if no debt whatever had been contracted in connection with it. If all the money spent by governments during the wars had been raised by taxes, but there had been the same destruction and failure to replace factories, houses, and other useful things, there would be exactly the same real burden on our children and grandchildren. It is on the wars that we must blame the destruction, not on the debt.

A more respectable argument is made by certain accountants who say that we have a false picture of how rich we are. They have suggested that every person, in order to get an accurate picture of how well off he is, ought to subtract from his visible wealth his share of the national debt. This would be a sound corrective for people who are prone to underestimate the burden of that part of his taxes, present and future, which is due to the existence of the national debt. But taxpayers are more prone to exaggerate than to underestimate these burdens, and even for those who underestimate this burden, counting their share of the national debt as an *additional* burden (however they may compute what is their share) would constitute a preposterous overcorrecting unless (a) they had counted the expected taxes as zero and (b) it was in fact decided to impose enough in taxes to pay off the whole national debt. Such calculations would not however make many people believe that the wealth at their disposal is really curtailed, so that not much harm could be done apart from the political effects of exaggerating the debit side of the national debt. This would hamper the development of rational policies in the incurring and the repayment of national debt.

After all this, it may seem as though we should just forget about the national debt, and simply write it off. If we owe it to ourselves, why bother to keep an account? The reason why the national debt cannot be simply repudiated is that the "we" does not indicate exactly the same people as the "ourselves." Although, *as a nation*, we owe the national debt to ourselves, some people owe more than they are owed; other people are owed more than they owe. Those who have a larger part of their wealth in the form of government securities than others would be hurt by a cancellation or repudiation of the national debt. We have persuaded them in the name of patriotism (often with dubious arguments) to buy government securities. It would be bad faith not to honor the national obligations to those who responded to the appeal.

Certain left-wingers maintain that the existence of national debt makes the rich richer and the poor poorer. They point out that most of the national debt belongs to rich people. (This of course is not surprising; after all, that is one reason why they are rich.) But everybody, including the poor, is taxed to provide the interest payments to the rich. On the other hand, right-wingers and rich people point out that rich people are taxed much more heavily than the poor, and that government bonds are owned by very large numbers of people most of whom are by no means rich.

Actually these two arguments more or less negate each other. The rich as a class would lose more than the poor from a repudiation of the bonds, but they would also gain more than the poor from the reduction in taxes that would accompany it. Just as a rich man gets much more in interest he also pays much more in taxes than a poor man. All in all it is doubtful whether the existence of the national debt has any appreciable effect on the relationship between the rich and the poor.

Now let us discuss the *real* effects of the national debt. The mere *existence* of the national debt has an effect on total spending. The people who own the national debt feel richer because of it and therefore they spend more money. Whether the extra spending is good or bad in its effect depends upon what the economy needs. If the economy is in a state of depression because there is not enough spending, then the extra spending brought about by the national debt is a good thing. It results in better business, more employment and a higher national income. But if there is enough spending to begin with, so that there is no depression, or if there is already too much spending so that the economy is suffering from inflationary pressures, the extra spending brought about by the national debt is a bad thing. It creates inflationary pressures or it increases them.

One way to stop people from spending too much is to increase taxes so that they have less money left to spend. This would not *really* impoverish them, whatever the individual taxpayer may feel about it, because all that the extra taxes would do would be to take away the extra money with which people were bidding up prices in trying to buy more than was available. After they pay the taxes, although they would be *spending* less, they would still be *buying* just as much as before but at lower prices. Only the *inflation* would be reduced by the extra taxation, not the quantities of goods and services that the public could actually obtain.

Nowadays governments for various reasons have to undertake large expenditures. There is at the same time so much expenditure for private consumption and private investment that if it were not for heavy taxes there would be too much spending and inflation. Since the existence of the national debt causes extra consumption, there must be more taxation to avoid inflation. Such additional taxation, although it does not constitute a subtraction from real income, does have harmful indirect effects which are discussed in Chapter XIV.

Even though it would be immoral to repudiate the national debt now that we have it, would it not have been better if we had not incurred it in the first place and so avoided these harmful indirect effects? What if the government had not spent the money or if it had raised the money by taxing instead of borrowing?

The answer is that our national income would have been less all throughout history, and not only by the amount of the national debt but by a multiple of that amount. Whenever the government (or any business or anybody else for that matter) spends money, income is created for the producers of what is bought. The income thus created results in more spending by those who have received it and this in turn creates extra income for still others so that the total income is increased by several times the initial increase in spending. The two hundred and ninety billion dollars of government spending (which was financed by the borrowing that built up the national debt to its present size) has thus resulted in contributing several times that amount to our total national income up to date—perhaps a thousand billion dollars. Without this two hundred and ninety billion dollars of government spending, and if no other spending had taken its place, we would have been in a really bad way. Some of the spending we could very well have done without, because there was at certain periods too much spending, which resulted in inflation. But without the income created directly and indirectly by the $290 billion of government expenditure we would have suffered from much longer and much deeper depressions throughout our history. Not only would we have consumed less over the period, but there would have been less investment too. We would today have fewer and poorer factories and roads and houses than we have. In real terms we would be much poorer, not richer.

Let us now suppose that the national income had been maintained all through history *without* creating any national debt—that private companies and corporations had spent money instead of the government with the same effect in maintaining income, consumption and investment; so that the real wealth of the country—its productive equipment—would be the same. We would then have no national debt. Would we be any better off?

Not at all. The expenditures by corporations and businesses and individuals would have built up private claims to wealth in exactly the same way that they have been built up by the national debt. American citizens would now own an extra two hundred and ninety billion dollars in shares of General Motors and other corporations. These shares would make them feel just as rich as government securities do (or perhaps richer inasmuch as dividend payments are generally higher than interest payments on national debt). We would therefore have the same extra spending or more. There would be exactly the same inflationary pressures and it would be just as necessary for the government to levy heavy taxes to prevent the inflation.

Our heavy taxes are made necessary by our great accumulation of private claims to wealth. These have the same effects whether they are in the form of national debt or whether they are in the form of ownership of property in businesses and corporations and houses. It is the ownership of claims to wealth which makes people spend more, and if this would otherwise lead to too much spending, there has to be more taxation to protect us from inflation. The blame lies not with the existence of national debt as such but with the existence of *any* claims to wealth.

This is, of course, no argument against increasing our national wealth. The benefits from an increase in wealth are certainly very much greater than the difficulties that accompany the increase.

Our conclusion is that we *do* owe the national debt to ourselves, that it is not a terrible danger to our society as imagined by those who think it is the same kind of thing as personal or inter-personal debt, and that there are some real problems, but that these problems are due to the existence and growth of *any* private claims to national wealth rather than of that part of private claims to wealth that are the counterpart of the national debt. These difficulties are connected with taxation which is the subject of the next chapter.

CHAPTER XIV

WHY TAXES?

It is generally supposed that the reason for taxes is that the government needs money to operate. This orthodox view seems sensible enough; and it fits in with the popular view of government as a kind of business. A business or household must earn money to meet expenses; the government must collect taxes for the same reason. A government can borrow money, but this should be done only temporarily and only for special occasions; just as for a household or for a business, for a government to overborrow is to risk bankruptcy. A government can create money, but this is seen as dangerous and corrupt, about as undesirable as counterfeiting, fraud or robbery.

In this analogy, taxation by a government corresponds to the earning of income through work by the individual; and the creation of money by the government corresponds to counterfeiting, fraud or robbery. But the analogy can be reversed and still be plausible. We could say that the government's *creating* money corresponds to the *earning* of money as an individual, and that taxation corresponds to robbery. After all, the creation of the money supply is a proper part of the duties of the government and taxation does consist of taking money away from people.

Such a reversal of the more usual analogy would, of course, outrage most people, but this is mainly because they are accustomed to thinking in other terms. The one analogy is just as legitimate as the other. People simply prefer the analogy which agrees with the ideas they hold to at the moment. This is why argument by analogy is inadequate and even dangerous. What really matters is the *effect* of a course of action, whether it be undertaken by a criminal, a business, a household, or a government. Let us forget, then, about the analogies and start to consider the *effects* of taxation by government.

The two most obvious effects of taxation are first, that the government acquires money; and second, that the taxpayer is left with less. But the government can acquire money by means that are much more convenient and much more pleasant than taxation. The government can borrow money; better still, it can print the money, or create it through the banks. Since these more pleasant ways of the government getting hold of some money are available, the government's need for money is not a good enough reason for imposing taxes. There must be better reasons if taxation is to be justified.

It should be noted that I am ignoring altogether the effects of the *spending* of money by the government. This is not because the effects of *spending* are unimportant, but only because they are exactly the same whether the government gets the money from taxation or by creating it. The effects of government spending can therefore be examined much more clearly when we have got out of the way the separate problem of which way the government gets its money.

For the taxpayer to have less money may be desirable in certain circumstances. A most important case of this is when there is excessive spending. The tax is then very useful because reducing the amount of money the taxpayer has causes him to spend less, thus correcting the excessive spending and preventing, moderating or curing the inflation. On the other hand, if spending is not enough to maintain full employment, then it is desirable to leave people with more money by *reducing* taxes.

If there is no inflationary or deflationary pressures to begin with, i.e., if total spending initially is "just right," and something caused the government to spend more money—say on military preparations —additional taxation is needed to stop inflation. Otherwise, people would be trying to purchase more goods and services than there were to be sold; the demand would be excessive. Given the same conditions, if government expenses decline, taxes should be *reduced* to stop deflation. Otherwise, people would not be able to buy all the goods and services available; the demand would be too low.

I am now saying that taxes must be increased whenever the government spends more, and decreased whenever the government spends less. This sounds very much like the proposition of orthodox finance that taxes must be collected to meet the expenses of the government. But it is not the same thing at all.

WHY TAXES?

Starting from a position with no inflationary or deflationary pressures, if the government must spend an additional $10 billion, taxes must indeed be increased. But they must be increased by *more* than the $10 billion, which the orthodox view would call for. If there were no increase in taxation at all, total spending would increase by much more than $10 billion. The $10 billion spent by the government constitutes extra income to the people who provide the extra goods and services bought by the government. These people will now spend the greater part of their $10 billion extra income on additional goods and services to consume. This induced spending creates additional income for those who produce the additional goods and services, these repercussions go on and on to bring about a total increase in spending, and thus in income, several times as great as the initial $10 billion increase in spending by the government. How much the total increase comes to depends on how great a proportion of the extra income is spent at each stage and how much is saved.

Let us suppose that the induced expenditure and income comes to $30 billion, so that the total effect of the government spending an extra $10 billion is a total increase in income of $40 billion. What would happen if taxes were increased by just as much as government spending was increased—i.e., by $10 billion? On the one hand the additional $10 billion spent by the government is earned by the public in providing the items bought by the government. On the other hand the $10 billion of additional taxation takes this amount away from them, so that they have neither more nor less income left after taxes than before. There is therefore no reason for expecting any change in spending by the public. The induced $30 billion of spending and income will have been eliminated. *But the original $10 billion of extra spending by the government is still there.* If there was no inflationary or deflationary pressure to begin with, i.e., if total spending was just at the right level to begin with, there will now be $10 billion too much spending and that much inflationary pressure. To prevent inflation it is therefore necessary to increase taxes by *more* than $10 billion—enough more to induce the public to spend $10 billion *less* than before, in spite of their earning the extra $10 billion spent by the government.

By how much taxes must be increased above the $10 billion mark to have this effect depends again on the spending-saving habits of the public. If the public cuts its spending by a large fraction of the reduction in its income after tax, a relatively small tax increase—one or two billions—will do the trick. The repercussions of the reduced spending in reducing other people's income, etc., will take care of the rest of the required $10 billion cut in spending. If the taxpayers resist reductions in consumptions more strongly, i.e., if they react to the tax increase more by reducing their saving and less by reducing their spending, a larger tax increase will be necessary. But in any case it is not sufficient to follow the orthodox principle of keeping the budget balanced (if it was balanced before) and increasing taxes by the same amount as government expenditure, taxes must be reduced by a larger amount if total expenditure is to be kept at the same level.

The policy of adjusting taxation and government spending to each other so as to keep total spending in the economy at the level needed to prevent both inflation and depression—even if it means unbalancing or overbalancing the government budget—is called "Functional Finance." It normally comes into conflict with orthodox or "Sound Finance" which maintains that the government should collect in taxes neither more nor less than it spends.

Some people attempt to follow both policies at the same time. They claim that while the government should balance its budget, collecting in taxes as much as it spends, it should also, if necessary, run a deficit to prevent a depression, or run a surplus to prevent inflation. But this really means *giving up* Sound Finance in favor of Functional Finance. On this approach Sound Finance would be followed and the budget would be balanced only when this is an unexpected and unplanned result of Functional Finance, i.e., only when according to Functional Finance there is no need for a deficit to prevent depression or for a surplus to prevent inflation. To make Sound Finance a genuine and effective guiding principle, one would have to give up Functional Finance and with it the objective of preventing depression and inflation. The principle of Sound Finance, or balancing the budget, is always either unnecessary or harmful. When Functional Finance balances the budget, the principle of Sound Finance is unnecessary; when Functional Finance would result in a deficit or a surplus, the principle of Sound Finance is harmful because it then permits inflation or depression.

WHY TAXES?

In this chapter we have been working on the assumption that inflation is caused only by excessive demand. In that case, unlike Sound Finance, Functional Finance, by keeping the level of demand no greater than is necessary for full employment, would protect the economy from inflation. But we have seen, in Chapter XI, that the economy can suffer from an inflation that is not caused by excessive demand, namely, sellers' inflation. If there are pressures that cause wages and prices to rise even when there is less than enough demand to provide full employment, even Functional Finance is not enough. Functional Finance is then unable to give us full employment and price stability at the same time but can be used only to maintain some compromise mixture of unemployment and sellers' inflation.

So far I have been speaking as if the only effect of taxation is that it takes money away from the taxpayer and thereby checks inflationary pressures. But this is not the only effect of taxation. We must examine the phenomenon of taxation anew to see how it works. Every tax is imposed either on some economic activity such as buying or selling something, or earning income, or inheriting property, or on some more passive economic *state* or condition such as owning property or simply living in a certain area. The activity or condition which renders a person subject to a tax I will call the "operation."

Every operation has a value or benefit to the person who performs it. The people who buy or sell or labor or accept an inheritance or live in a particular place do so because of the benefit from the operation. If the benefit is greater than the tax the operation is still carried on in spite of the tax because there is still some benefit left. If the tax is greater than the benefit, however, the operation is abandoned. The purchase or the sale is not made, the work is not done, the income is not earned, the inheritance is not accepted, the home is given up.

It is important to note that in the latter case, i.e., where the tax is greater than the benefit and the operation is abandoned, no tax is collected. The government does not have more money, neither does the public as a whole have less money. But there is still an important effect. Everybody who has had an operation eliminated by being made subject to the tax has been made worse off. Even if he finds himself with *more money* (because the tax has eliminated a purchase he would have made) he has lost the benefit from the eliminated purchase. At the same time the would-be seller, who finds himself with *less money,* has lost his benefit from the eliminated sale.

A tax which at every point where it applies is greater than the benefit, so that its only effect is to eliminate operations, can be justified only if it is intended to stop the operations as morally or socially undesirable. It is equivalent to a *prohibition* of the operations rather than to a tax since no money passes from any taxpayer to the government. The individuals affected—whether they are would-be buyers or would-be sellers or would-be workers or would-be savers or would-be inheritors or residents or what not—are made worse off by being prevented from doing something that they wanted to do. Such a tax reduces the efficiency of the economy. It prevents the economy from providing individuals with the things they want.

At the other end of the scale is the tax which at no point is greater than the benefit from the operation. This tax never eliminates any operation. It therefore does no harm to the efficiency of the economy but only transfers money from the taxpayers to the government. There is then no social loss. It is true that the taxpayer is made poorer by having to pay the tax: but this may be exactly the purpose of the tax—either to make him poorer only in *money* terms in order to reduce spending and prevent an inflation, when he will be able to buy just as much with his remaining money; or to make him poorer in *real* terms because he is considered to be too rich.

It is, however, very difficult to find taxes which are nowhere greater than the benefit—and which therefore do no damage to the efficiency of the economy. The nearest thing to such a "socially harmless" tax is the tax on the rent of land. If the tax simply takes a percentage of the rent of the land, the landlord will still rent the land to the user who pays the most (and who presumably puts it to the most profitable use which is at the same time the socially most important use). The landlord will do this because it still yields him the greatest possible return *net* of tax. The rent can never be more than the benefit to the user from renting the land, other-

WHY TAXES?

wise he would not pay it, and a tax of less than 100% of the rent is clearly less than the benefits, so that no operation is eliminated and the tax is socially harmless.

Some people became so enthusiastic about the tax on land rents that they wanted to make it the *only* tax and are called "single taxers." A long time ago such a tax might possibly have been sufficient. But not nowadays. Even 100% tax on all land rents would be far from sufficient to prevent inflation.

The problems of taxation arise from the fact that any tax law that can be framed has a different impact on different people and on different units of the same operation for the same people. Up to a certain point, say, in the purchase of a particular taxed commodity, that is to say for a certain number of units of it, the benefit is greater than the tax. These units continue to be bought in spite of the tax so that no operation is eliminated and no social harm is done. But beyond this point, i.e., for additional units of the item, the benefit is less than the tax and the further units are not bought. Here the operation *is* eliminated, no tax is collected, and the efficiency of the economy is harmed.

An ideal tax is one which operates only in the first way. (A tax which applied only to the pure rent on pure land, i.e., none of it being paid for anything done by man to improve the land, would qualify as perfect in this sense. Hence the "single taxers.") But no actual tax could be ideal in this sense. Other taxes which are definitely not ideal are therefore necessary and our problem is to find those that do the least damage to the economy. If the purpose of the tax is to take money away from people and not to eliminate certain economic "operations" this analysis provides a criterion of how good or how bad a tax is. A tax is a better tax the less the destruction of benefits in relation to the amount of money collected.

Inheritance and income taxes are perhaps the least harmful. But inheritance taxes may induce a person to "eliminate the operation" of leaving an inheritance, i.e., it may induce him to spend his wealth before he dies so as to avoid the inheritance tax rather than have the government take away a large part of it when he dies.

The income tax was for a long time considered to be almost ideal in our sense. It was argued that since a properly designed income tax would always leave a larger net income after tax out of a larger gross income before tax, businessmen interested in maximizing the net income after tax would still maximize their profits, or gross income before tax, so that the working of the economy would not be interfered with. But, as we have seen, a man may refuse to do extra work because the tax on it makes it not worth his while. The income tax, then, though it does not discriminate between different ways of earning money, all subject to the same income tax, does discriminate between working and enjoying leisure. There is no tax on leisure: there *is* a tax on money earned from extra work. If the tax stops us from doing a certain piece of work, we lose the benefit we would have got from it and the government gets nothing. This is a social loss.

Opponents of income taxes, or of taxes in general, frequently declare that taxes are too heavy and that they have passed or are about to pass some critical level which they call "the point of diminishing returns" or "taxable capacity." These phrases do not seem to have any recognizable meaning, but they are rhetorically and politically very impressive. They were much in use recently when there was a movement for a constitutional amendment to limit taxes to 25% of an individual's income. This proposal was confused with a pronouncement by a famous economist-statistician, Mr. Colin Clark, that a rate of taxation of more than 25% is damaging to the effectiveness of the economy, although Mr. Colin Clark was speaking of the percentage of the *total national income* taken in taxes and not of the percentage of the income of a very rich man. It is not so long since it was fashionable to say that ten percent is the largest part of the national income which can safely be taken away in taxes, and in the history books we read that the feeling against an income tax of one percent of *anybody's* income was much stronger than the feeling now against the income taxes which go as high as 91% on the excess of income over $200,000. There are no simple rules about the limits of taxation, even though an arbitrary number can be made to sound impressive by calling it the "point of diminishing returns" or the "taxable capacity" of the economy.

It is frequently claimed that high income tax rates discourage investors. Investors are reluctant to risk their money if the possible

WHY TAXES?

profit is so severely reduced that investment becomes a "heads you win, tails I lose" proposition. At the same time we hear of business being charged with undertaking excessively risky investments on the theory that they do not care very much if money is lost because the losses can be subtracted from other earnings, thus reducing taxes.

The two arguments obviously cancel out. The government does take a large share of any profits, but where the investor, private or corporate, is making large enough profits on other ventures, the government also pays a large share of any losses (in the form of tax reductions) leaving the investment neither more attractive nor less attractive. If a million dollars is invested in a venture and it fails, a million dollars is subtracted from other profits subject to tax, reducing taxes by, say, $500,000. The government then in fact pays 50% of the loss. On the other hand, if the investment turns out well, the government takes 50% of the profits. The corporation therefore acts as if it is in partnership with the government on a 50-50 basis.

High rates of taxation on income or profits have been charged with leading us surreptitiously into socialism. The theory is that a high tax rate makes business unprofitable, resulting in a low rate of private investment and unemployment. The government then takes steps, like government investment, to alleviate the unemployment, financing its activity by borrowing, thus increasing the national debt. The increased national debt calls for additional interest payments, and the government consequently increases taxes still further to raise the money for the interest payments. The higher taxes in turn make private investment still less profitable so that there is still more unemployment and still more borrowing is undertaken by the government to finance its measures for alleviating unemployment. Thus the whole economy becomes "socialist" quite by accident (although it is usually insinuated that some cunning conspirators have planned it that way all along behind the scenes).

This intriguing argument embraces almost all the fallacies that I have been trying to uncover in this book. We have just seen that a high tax rate, while it reduces the net profits of the investor, also reduces the risk of loss, because the investor can subtract losses from other profits and so pay less taxes.[1]

This does not hold for investors who do not have other profits from which the losses can be subtracted for tax purposes. They do not enjoy complete "loss offset." The proper solution for this is to make the loss offset more general so that all investors, including small investors, could enjoy the benefits that are now enjoyed by large and prosperous corporations who do have other profits against which they can offset the losses.

The simplest and most effective way to make "loss offset" perfectly general is for the government to pay out a subsidy (a negative tax) on *all* losses at the same rate as the positive tax on all profits. Such a procedure would not have the effect, as might be thought, of encouraging investors to make foolish investments in order to earn the subsidy paid on losses. If the subsidy on losses is at the same rate as the tax on profits it would merely offset the discouragement to risky investment that is caused by the tax on profits and restore the right balance between enterprise and caution. However, a subsidy on losses sounds so revolutionary that it can be applied only when it can be disguised as a "deduction" or "refund" as is the present practice, even though such a restriction discriminates unfairly against those who do not have other profits from which they can deduct the losses.

Nor is it true that any investment the government might undertake in order to cure unemployment must be financed by borrowing. The government can increase demand by increasing both its expenditure and its taxation equally, keeping the budget balanced, and there will be an increase in total spending equal to the increase in the size of the budget as shown in Chapter XIII. There is also the possibility of the government's financing the increase in employment by the creation of new money. This would not mean inflation, because the extra spending here would be absorbed in offsetting the deflation.

Furthermore, even if the government should borrow to finance

---

[1] The large corporations which have been spending much money advertising the bad effects of heavy taxes on investment are, indeed, taking advantage of this very thing in making the government pay, in reduced taxes, a large part of the cost of such advertisements.

its full employment measures there is no necessity for taxes to be increased to pay the interest on the increased national debt. The interest payment can be met by further borrowing or by money creation. And finally all of these things could be done by a government which religiously kept its hands off any type of business in which private enterprise is in the least interested.

It is clear then that high taxes do not necessarily imply the replacement of private enterprise by government enterprise. Nevertheless, a high rate of taxation *is* closely related to socialism—even more closely than is suggested by the argument I have just criticized. If a government collects fifty per cent of the profits of business, in taxes, and because of "loss offset," also carries fifty per cent of the losses, it is just as if the government owned fifty per cent of the business. Indeed, if by socialism we mean the *effect* of government ownership of production facilities, rather than the legal title or actual management, we do already have considerable socialism. The high tax rates can more properly be said to *be* socialism than to *threaten* it.

To some people the recognition of this socialistic development will seem catastrophic. To others it will sound like the partial achievement of a great ideal. But the true lesson is that if we could become so largely socialist without noticing it at all, then it cannot matter much either for good or for evil. The word socialism should not prejudice us to believe that what has happened is per se either good or bad. To the contrary, we should only consider whether or not the changes that have taken place have benefited or harmed the people in our country. We must remember that economics, which is *everybody's business,* is not primarily about capitalism or socialism but about people. The real test of any economic event or policy is always: "Does it help or does it hinder people in getting what they consider good for themselves?"

CHAPTER XV

POLITICAL ECONOMY OR THE USE OF ECONOMICS*

How can economics serve to control human behavior? Should it do so? For what purpose? These are the questions I would like to consider here.

In one sense economics neither has nor can have a purpose of its own: it is the study of ways in which people can succeed in achieving their purposes. The economist does not ask what these purposes may be; he is concerned only with the means and methods. Economics has been defined as the study of the allocation of scarce means among alternative ends, and it is not an accident that no mention is made of what the alternative ends might be. The economist as economist can never criticize the ends: he can only criticize means for achieving them; and he can criticize these only by the criterion of their efficiency in achieving the given ends.

But in another sense, in refusing to take any position as to the ends themselves, and leaving it entirely to the individual to choose what he wants to get, or to the group which has somehow arranged to work together as an individual, the economist is silently accepting a most important end—the end of letting individuals decide freely for themselves what they want. The economist then devotes himself to considering how this end can be achieved most efficiently. This idea has been expressed by saying that the economist is basically interested in the maximization of freedom.

The economist is, of course, interested in achieving the greatest possible production of the goods and services the individual would like to have. This is in itself a matter of increasing a man's freedom, in the sense that he is free to enjoy more of the things that he wants

---

* This chapter is based on a paper presented at a conference on Modern Knowledge and the Control of Man held at the New School for Social Research, and was published in the *American Scholar* (Summer 1960, pp. 377-385) under the title "Economics and the Control of Man."

instead of suffering the oppression of doing without them. But the economist is concerned with freedom in a more basic sense. He is concerned with discovering to what extent it is possible to let one individual have more of what he wants *without taking anything away from anyone else*. This is the kind of efficiency that really can be said to work toward increasing human freedom to the highest degree.

If the end of economics is the maximization of human freedom, it would be something of a paradox if it used "controls" to do this, for the essence of freedom is the absence of controls. I have been in trouble with this paradox a number of times ever since I wrote a book called *The Economics of Control*. Many readers of this book have been disappointed because I do not discuss controls in the most obvious sense of restrictions on men's freedom to choose their occupations, their residences, the prices they are permitted to pay or to receive for goods and services, or the quantities they are permitted to buy or to sell. There are, of course, those who are concerned not with the freedom or even the welfare of the people affected, but with the freedom of the controller, or of a controlling group or elite, to use controls to fashion society, or even humanity, in accordance with certain ideals or messianic objectives. More often there is nothing more sinister about the interest in controls than the feeling that some special situation calls for controls instead of the normal uncontrolled procedures of free markets, or a dislike for the market system, or a failure to understand it. Whatever current dilemma we find ourselves in always seems to be in some way different, so that there is always an excuse for imposing controls in the name of some emergency.

It is hard for me to remember, but it is possible that in 1932, when I first thought of writing *The Economics of Control,* I too had a prejudice favoring regulation by authorities. Or there may be other explanations of my having chosen the word "control." Anyway, over many years, in the course of learning more economics and writing the book, the meaning of the word changed subtly and it was softened. "Control" came to mean to me not commands to people to act in a certain way, but institutions that caused men to behave in a desired way without feeling that they were being deprived of their freedom, and indeed, without their really *being* deprived of it. The great paradox is rather that the economist was concerned with understanding the operation of institutions that caused men *freely* to behave in such ways as to achieve the end of increasing every individual's opportunities for doing what he preferred or getting what he wanted. There are situations in which people can be forced to be free, such as those in which laws command them to keep to the right of the road so that they are free to drive with much more safety. The *economic* institutions are those by which people are not forced but induced to do of their own free will what is needed to guarantee freedom in general.

The high prestige that economics enjoys among the social sciences is a result of its success in discovering and explaining the dynamics of several vital processes: how the market mechanism can work to induce the resources of the world to be harnessed to the production and distribution of the goods and services that consumers want; how this is achieved through the unintended collaboration toward this purpose of millions of people who are directly concerned for the most part only with earning a living for themselves and their families; how these millions of people find they can achieve their private ends by doing just the things that are useful for the "social purpose" of helping to provide complete strangers in distant parts of the world with the goods and services that they desire.

Many of the most celebrated economic principles prove to be tautologies whose real contents do not match their external splendor. And this can also be applied to some of the reasons cited for the success of economics as compared with her sister social sciences. The real reason for this success is to be found in the nature of social problems that are counted as "economic." Many times some social action is proposed that is in the general interest, or at least in the interest of what appears to be the majority, but there are some who do not like the results and will not agree to it. To coerce them is considered to be immoral, or too expensive, or dangerous, and so the social action is held up until some way is discovered, or invented, to make it possible for the general consent to be achieved. This means that some device must be developed for compensating the objectors, while retaining some of the net benefit all around. When such a device is not found possible, there remains a conflict of interest, and the problem is a political one. Where it *has* been found possible to develop such a device, and a set of institutions has been built up for the regular achievement of such compensation, the problem is declared to be an economic one. Economics is the successful social science because those problems which have been solved successfully are declared to be economic problems. The conflicting interests have been reduced to some common measure, usually money, and full compensation can be paid wherever the benefits from the proposed action are greater than the damages. The solved problem then falls naturally into the realm of social problems to which the measuring rod of money is applicable, namely the realm of economics.

Money and the market are the institutions by which people are induced, or tempted, or bribed, to do what is in the social interest. If this is control, it is a subtle, a gentle, even if very effective, form of control in which the controllees have the illusion of not being controlled but free. One may argue that the donkey who follows the carrot (and who regularly gets one) only *feels* more free than the donkey who flees the stick (and who regularly gets that). But could it not be that this is all that is meant by saying he *is* more free? Is not freedom, after all, essentially an illusion?

The true heroes of the maximization of freedom in our economy were not the classical economists. These merely discovered the nature of the operations of the price mechanism in harnessing the private interests of producing and providing things that people wanted and getting them to the places where they wanted them. The true heroes were the preclassical *political economists* who developed the institutions that made it possible for the system to work, going back to the ancient solons who developed the institution of private property and then corporate property, who established the rule of law that gave security to property and the freedom of individuals to move and to trade. The classical economists, although they were also political economists in concerning themselves with governmental economic policies for the further development and refinement of economic institutions for maximizing freedom, were primarily concentrating on explaining the "natural" working of the system thus developed. This was especially true around the end of the nineteenth century and the beginning of the twentieth, when the system seemed to be working pretty well and required little tampering. That is why it seemed appropriate for the name of the discipline to be changed from "political economy" to "economics." The implication was that economists were basically concerned with studying some fundamental or universal aspects of the nature of the world and of men, a study that had more in common with physics than with politics.

In part this was a natural reaction to the annoying stupidities of sentimental socialists or anticapitalists who had no understanding of the complex and subtle machinery that made modern life possible, and who had eyes only for flaws in the operation of the economy of the present and wished only to contrast it with idealized utopias of the future. In part it was a natural reaction to the even more annoying vaporings of opponents of unromantic industrialism and calculating rationalism who believed in imaginary golden ages of the past. But the resulting over-concentration of economists on the aesthetic perfections of perfect competition led to the elevation of the absence of any sort of control, of *laissez faire*, from an extraordinarily effective instrument that was a part of the whole economic system, to a sacred principle of social organization—from a piece of machinery that must be judged by its efficacy in achieving the desired ends of society, to a moral imperative.

In recent decades such pious worship of *laissez faire* has become less and less possible as the responsibility of government for more and more social objectives has come to be taken for granted. The alleviation of poverty, the provision of public health services, the furnishing of education for all on higher and higher levels, the responsibility for the availability of more elaborate and more essential communication services, and the massive equalization of income and of wealth by progressive taxation—all go to make up what might be called the revolution of our time, were not the word usually reserved for more spectacular but less important changes in the life of man in society. And now so vast has become the government's necessary expenditures for defense, in addition to all these other activities, that it is almost impossible, but alas not quite impossible, for people in authority to be unaware of the way in which the financial activities of the government impinge on the economy. The government cannot evade the responsibility for so directing these programs as to keep the totality of economic activities in the country from generating the evils of inflation on the one hand, and of depression, or perhaps I should say recession, on the other.

It is almost a quarter of a century since Lord Keynes (and the Great Depression) clarified the role that the government of a modern state must play in keeping total expenditure in the economy, private and governmental, at the level required for full employment without inflation, by appropriate monetary and fiscal policies. When there is too little spending, with consequent unemployment, the monetary authorities can encourage business to spend more on investment and the public to spend more on consumption by an expansionary monetary policy. Such a policy increases the money supply and makes credit easier (by lowering interest rates), thus increasing total spending and employment. When too much spending causes an inflation, the monetary authorities can check or prevent this by a restrictive monetary policy. This policy decreases the money supply and makes credit tighter (by raising interest rates), thereby inducing business to spend less on investment and the public to spend less on consumption.

The government can also reduce total spending by a restrictive fiscal policy, that is, by spending less itself or by increasing taxes so that taxpayers will have less left to spend after taxes; it can increase total spending by an expansionary fiscal policy, by spending more itself or reducing taxes so that taxpayers will have more left to spend.

In choosing between these different instruments for regulating total spending, the government would naturally take account of the condition of the economy, which sometimes makes one of these instruments more effective and sometimes another. The government's choice would also be influenced by its preference as to which of the different kinds of spending to change, using monetary policy when it preferred to influence private investment more, and varying certain taxes if it preferred to change private consumption, unless it preferred to modify its own spending program. But despite the way these secondary considerations determined the details of its monetary and fiscal policies, the government could still apply its monetary and fiscal policies so as to maintain continuous prosperity.

At the present time this painfully learned lesson seems to be in great danger of being forgotten or perhaps rejected. This has made the relearning of the lesson, with some changes that will prevent the recurrence of the same crisis, a matter of the utmost importance for the persistence of free society.

I am aware that this is a strong statement, and that I am to be suspected, and properly, of exaggerating the importance of my own discipline; but I am convinced that this is not a crisis for the economics profession but for the economy at large. Indeed, the failure to solve the economic problems of society is the highroad to success for the profession of teaching economics, for in times of prosperity interest in economics drops sharply. It is when the economy is in the throes of depression or inflation that it seems important to study economics and the profession booms—at least as long as the economy remains viable. The crisis is one of free society as a whole, and it would be wrong indeed if I allowed a professional modesty to curb my wish to speak out about it.

What has happened since the path-breaking work of Keynes is that a new element has entered the picture that he did not foresee, although it is possible now, with the benefit of hindsight, to point to some clues that could have been seen even in his time. This new element is the growth of the power of large corporations and of powerful trade unions to increase the prices of the product or of the labor that they sell, *even in times of considerable depression and incomplete utilization of capacity.* Instead of inflation being caused only by the pressure of buyers trying to buy more goods and services that the economy can produce, so that it is always a "buyers' inflation," it is now possible to have inflation even when this is not the case—even when the output of the economy is far below capacity and there is substantial unemployment. We also can have "sellers' inflation," when prices are raised by the pressure of sellers.

With this development, attempts to stop a sellers' inflation by restrictive fiscal or monetary measures, which would be the appropriate cure if it were a buyers' inflation, only brings about depression. Attempts to cure this depression by expansionary monetary or fiscal policies only restore the sellers' inflation. The resulting frustrations have induced a regression to a pre-Keynesian worship of a balanced government budget as a charm against the bedevilment of inflation in the midst of recession. Instead of the budget being used as an instrument for balancing the other expenditures in the economy so as to maintain prosperity, prosperity is sacrificed, as in ancient (i.e., pre-Keynesian) times, to the fetish of a balanced budget, and the economy continues to suffer from sellers' inflation moderated by induced depression.

In an affluent society such as ours, which could waste 10 per cent or more of its productive resources and still give the unemployed a bearable standard of living, this could be accepted with some equanimity were we not living in the crucial years of the Communist challenge for title to the planet. One can hardly call it a race, for the free world is barely running. With a few billions of dollars, or perhaps tens of billions of dollars per annum, we could help the uncommitted millions of Asia, Africa and Latin America, to raise their standards of living rapidly enough to make freedom meaningful to them, but we are told that we cannot afford it. Additional expenditures on defense might save the world from destruction by protecting the Russians from the temptation of thinking they could destroy our retaliatory power by a first blow (to which the rules of the game entitle them), but we are told we cannot afford that. And we are told this while we are complacently losing some thirty to fifty billion dollars a year from the induced depression, and spending perhaps one hundred billion dollars a year on goods that we need so little that we have to spend another ten billion in persuading ourselves to buy them. The balanced budget (or rather the declaration of intent to balance the budget) is not merely a symptom —it is a powerful tranquilizer. Widely representative of this frightening complacency, except for its unusual openness, is the response of a woman interviewed recently over television. Asked by Dave Garroway what she thought of the United States position vis à vis Russia on intercontinental and extra-planetary rockets, she said that the United States had always been and would always be first in everything. When Garroway pointed out that we were not first in outer space, he was met with, "Give us time!"

The apparent political success of such gambling with the future of free society on the chance that we *will* be given time will continue as long as we fail to realize that what we really cannot afford is to check a sellers' inflation by engineering depression. We must check the sellers' inflation directly by preventing administered prices and administered wages from being so handled that they cause sellers' inflation. This means stopping such increases in the general wage level as cannot be met out of increased productivity or reduced profit margins, and stopping such increases in prices of products as cannot be offset by price reductions elsewhere.

Even though such controls need involve no threat to the freedom of individuals and no sanctions more grievous than the elimination of certain tax privileges, there will be strong resistances. But the government cannot evade its responsibility by hiding behind a balanced budget (or the hope of an apparently balanced window-dressing of a budget). Nor can this responsibility be evaded by an unwillingness to see that while we are merely recovering some lost ground, the Russians are increasing their output rapidly and the Chinese promise to grow at an even more rapid pace if they can overcome the stresses of the introduction of a still more violent exploitation of human capacity for toil.

When I say that we may be witnessing in our lifetime the failure of the free world to withstand the totalitarian onslaught, it is not my language but the objective situation that is melodramatic. We may fail because we are unprepared to make the effort needed and because we are using the superstition of the primacy of a balanced budget to excuse the failure to make the effort. Economic knowledge, by re-exploding this reincarnation of an old fallacy, and by showing how the authorities can avoid sellers' inflation as well as buyers' inflation, can set us free to apply our vast resources for the defense of the free world and the economic development of the poor world in our fight with the totalitarian world. This is the task and this is the case for political economy.